SWATCHWAY MAGIC

PAUL ANTROBUS & CHARLES SCOONES

With guest chapters by
RICHARD MATTHEWS & DICK DURHAM

Introduction by BOB FISHER

A collection of contemporary yarns around the East Coast Swatchways of Essex and Suffolk by water and by land

Magical

Go there, be there and the magic is yours to enjoy

DELANCEY PRESS
LONDON 2012

Published by Delancey Press Ltd
23 Berkeley Square,
London W1J 6HE

www.delanceypress.co.uk

PHOTOGRAPHS and the MAP
Most of the photographs are originals by Charles Scoones ©Charles Scoones
Some are by Paul Antrobus ©Paul Antrobus
The map was created by Charles Scoones ©Charles Scoones
The photographs in Chapter 15, 'Growing up on the East Coast', are from Richard Matthews' own archive and subject to individual copyrights.

Typeset by BookType
Printed and bound in Great Britain by 4edge Ltd, Hockley.

A CIP catalogue record for this title is available from the British Library

ISBN 978-1-907205-17-0

First published 2012

"A beguiling chronicle"

By Captain Richard Woodman

In the years since the Second World War sailing has become a popular sport and past-time, enjoyed by many people from all walks of life. One highly influential figure in this transformation was Maurice Griffiths, a yacht-designer, small-boat sailor, journalist of distinction and sometime editor of 'Yachting Monthly'. In 1932 Griffiths published his third book, 'The Magic of the Swatchways', which advocated cruising the creeks, rivers and inlets fringing the Thames Estuary.

Griffiths' book is arguably one of the most influential sailing books written in English, painting a powerfully compelling picture of these waters that penetrate deep into the countryside of an England most have forgotten exists. Both Paul Antrobus and Charles Scoones fell under its spell when young men, coming to love these bleak yet beautiful tidal waters.

Late in their lives, still active small-boat enthusiasts, they set out to see what remained of the magic so readily evoked by Griffiths and found that, despite the explosion of popular sailing and the existence of moorings almost anywhere a boat can float, even if only at high-tide, much of the magical quality of cruising these waters still exists.

In a series of voyages, assisted by the accounts and contributions of similarly inclined friends – including Griffiths' biographer – Antrobus and Scoones recount in this book their return to their roots as yachtsmen.

It is a beguiling chronicle that persuades me, writing this in the depth of winter, to fit out my own boat and set off for a lonely anchorage where only the piping of the foraging oyster-catchers can disturb the tranquillity of a peaceful evening.

Richard Woodman aboard his yacht 'Andromeda' passing the clubroom window at Walton & Frinton Yacht Club

Captain Richard Woodman FRHistS FNI
Elder Brother of Trinity House
Naval historian and novelist

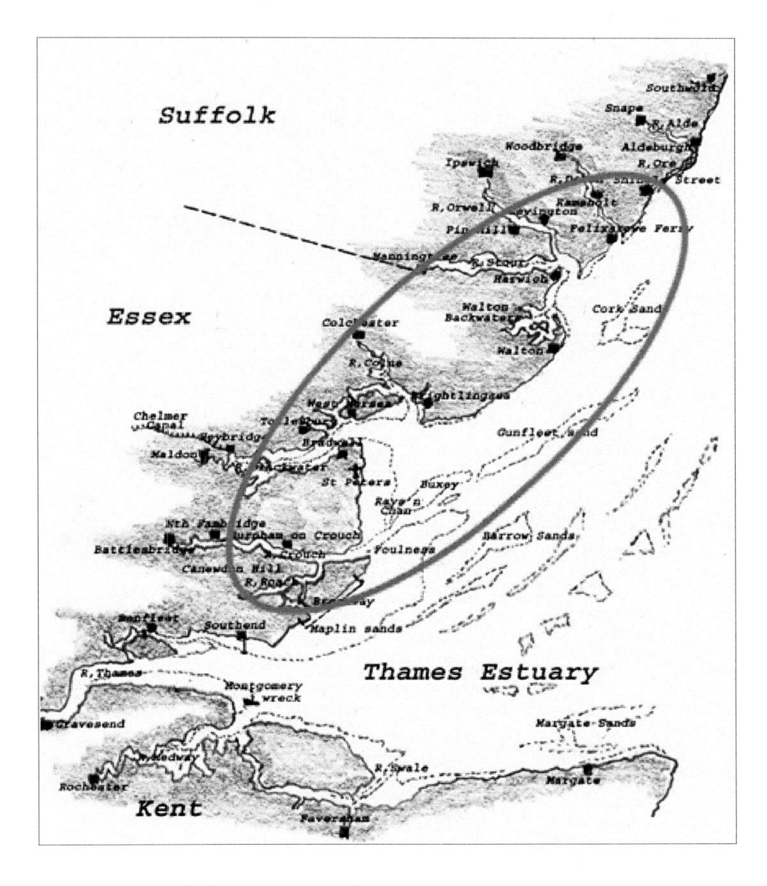

If you would like a copy of the Swatchways map (without the red lozenge) or any of the Scoones/Antrobus images for your personal use, please email to swatchways@aquafirma.com.

A charge will be made for production and postage depending on what is requested.

Contents

Introduction

Once a Bricklesey boy, always...

By Bob Fisher, veteran sailor, yachting author and journalist and born and bred in Brightlingsea

'Swatchway Magic' is about my roots, too, and I like the way you can dip into this book at any chapter for a short story and be encouraged that the sailing and the scenery are still all there. Great fun reading about it all again

For I am a 'Bricklesey boy' and justly proud of it, as are many others. As a small boy, I used to listen to the tales of the old men of the foreshore, gathered in the fishermen's shelter at the top of the hard. It was from them, men with 'Shamrock' or 'Endeavour' or other magical names emblazoned across their jerseys, that I first learned about the America's Cup – they had been there.

The most senior among them was the father of my mother's best friend, 'Lucky' Jack Linder. Jack had been aboard 'Shamrock III' when she raced the gigantic sloop 'Reliance' for the Cup in 1903. His stories were fantastic to a boy of 10. These days, when I am in New Zealand, chasing the latest twist in an America's Cup story, I endeavour to meet up with his grandson, Robin Linder, who after more than 50 years in the Land of the Long White Cloud still claims to be a 'Bricklesey boy'.

My daughter recently gave me 'The Log of Velsa', published in 1920 and written by prolific author and playwright Arnold Bennett, wherein he said, "East Anglia, including North Essex, is as English as any part of England, and more English than most...Angles took possession of it very early in history and probably no place is more Anglian than Brightlingsea". He also said it is never pronounced as it is written, quoting, "Dr Edward Percival Dickin, the historian of the town, has found 193 different ways of spelling the name." In my probably later edition by the same historian, dated 1939, he claims, "the different spellings number 404."

Bennett also wrote, "Smuggling was an important industry at Brightlingsea, and to suppress it laws were passed making it illegal to construct fast rowing or sailing boats." Luckily, this had changed by the time I began my sailing in Brightlingsea in a variety of boats, from a 'converted' oyster skiff with home-made spars and sails to several years in the Brightlingsea One-Design class. Speed, however, began to rear its ugly head and I went for the new-fangled planing dinghies. The Hornet was my first love but I was game for anything fast and moved into catamarans with the late, legendary Reg White, a friend since we were pushed out in prams alongside one another by our mothers.

I spent most of the summer of 1967 on a sabbatical

leave from the BBC, working with Reg to develop the Tornado. It was important for his business, Sailcraft, that we had it as close to perfection as possible for the trials at Sheppey to select a boat suitable for international racing. Reg and I sailed the prototype to a clear victory. The Tornado was chosen and later became an Olympic class at the Montreal Games in 1976 where Reg and his brother-in-law, John Osborn, won gold medals.

Their triumph prompted a riotous open-topped bus tour of honour around the town and two MBEs awarded in the next honours list. It is bizarre that for the UK home-based Olympics in 2012, the multihull category was dropped completely from the Olympic sailing classes. But the history isn't lost.

The catamaran ethos was strong in Brightlingsea from the beginning of the 60s, begun as I remember by Roy Bacon who sought Reg's help to build his first boat. The progress was fast into the C-Class cats and, with them, the International Catamaran Challenge which became colloquially known as the 'Little America's Cup'.

Originally GB v USA match races, like the original America's Cup proper, GB won continuously from the first in 1961 until 1968. Reg took the helm from 1963 to 1966 and again in 1968 with three 'Hellcats', two 'Emma Hamiltons' and then, for three occasions from 1966, with 'Lady Helmsman'. I was fortunate enough to be his crew in 1967. 'Lady Helmsman' sported a wing mast/sail rig. Now all the talk for the America's Cup proper is of catamarans and wing masts so 'Oracle Racing' is hardly breaking new ground. It's just 45 years too late – or the 'Brightlingsea boys' would be in there with a strong chance of winning!

I wrote my first book, 'Catamaran Racing', with Reg

White. It is alleged that he told the publisher, Ken Parker of Cassell's, "I'm virtually illiterate, but legitimate. Bob, on the other hand, is literate and a bit of a bastard." On such introductions are great works created!

As I stood at the memorial to Reg at the top of the hard in late December – 'Reg's Rock' they call it – I paused to wonder what Arnold Bennett would have thought of Brightlingsea today. I looked to the fishermen's shelter, newly painted, for reassurance that the past was not all lost and then at Grandfather Percival's Anchor Hotel, which no longer serves beer or offers casual accommodation to the traveller. On the other side, the shipyard and its slipways have been replaced by flats and houses.

And then I cast my eyes towards the Creek and Cindery Island and my own plentiful and happy memories came flooding back. Bennett would have approved of what I saw, looking seaward, at least, and I suspect so would have Maurice Griffiths.

In our youth we spread our wings by going to local regattas and open meetings at West Mersea, Stone and

"Looking across Brightlingsea Creek and Cindery Island, happy memories come flooding back"

Tollesbury in Hornets, Enterprises and Fireballs. They were always great regattas, particularly the Tollesbury Gooseberry Pie Fayre, and we were a boisterous gang of crews at the evening parties.

Although I moved almost 40 years ago to live on the South Coast, to sail elsewhere and to write books about the America's Cup and the chronicles of the Whitbread/ Volvo round the world races, when I return from time to time to Brightlingsea I get that same feeling that the writers of this little book are talking about...home.

Enjoy the reading! Better still, get to the Swatchways they write about and enjoy the magic at first hand.

Bob Fisher
December 2011

Prologue

Intertwining Swatchways yarns – where to and why

PAUL ANTROBUS TRAVELS ACROSS EIGHT DECADES

This compendium was inspired by Maurice Griffiths' famous book 'The Magic of the Swatchways'. Charles and I are not trying to recreate the sea passages he described 80 years ago but simply to revisit the territory to see for ourselves if the magic is still there.

We cover the same Essex and Suffolk coastal waters in modern, comfortable boats – under sail, under power and sometimes reconnoitering by road – going to all the places MG sailed to. But he stayed aboard mainly while we venture ashore to enjoy the pubs and sights and entertainment that now abound there – maybe always did.

Much has changed in sailing boats since MG wrote 'The Magic of the Swatchways'. In that narrative, MG sailed the area in several different yachts, mostly around 32ft, mostly gaff rigged, some yawls, nearly all much loved but often with serious faults in their sailing ability.

MG and his crews loved solitude and took on many challenges, not always working the tides as they should. They would beat into big seas off Clacton against the tide, for instance, taking forever to clear the pier and not making any real progress until the tide turned, but seemingly unable to turn away from the wind.

Unlike many boats today which are efficient on all points of sailing, they were hard to reef, hard to handle and recurring tales involved getting very wet below. "What a night that was!" was an oft repeated phrase. Every trip seemed to present testing moments but there were always periods of optimism and, especially, extreme pleasure expressed at the anchorage made and comfortably tucked into. "The smell of sizzling from the galley..." is a theme that always seemed to make a bad trip OK.

MG recorded a comment he made in conversation with one crew: "There's something mysterious about these deserted creeks and tiny islands that you never get in the Solent. There's scarcely a sound, is there?"

In these same creeks we still find peaceful anchorages or noisy, convivial pubs ashore where chatter dominates rather than piped music. The old salt in the Butt & Oyster, Pin Mill, says, "We've seen changes but what we do is much the same – we go sailing," and the stories flow.

The tides still have to be worked. The places are as pretty as Constable paintings. The foreshore teems with life as the tide recedes and returns with lapping ripples.

This is our personal collection of stories of the Swatchways, not necessarily sequential or chronological but interwoven with each other like a Turk's Head knot to create a picture of these waters as we find them now. We describe how we navigated some of our voyages, buoys and all, but not as a pilot guide. For that and safe sailing you can't do better than a current edition of 'East Coast Rivers', published as part of the Wiley Nautical 'Cruising Companion' series.

The places are as endearing as ever. The people still have real life yarns to tell. The ancient Broomway across the Maplin Sands still links Saxon-time sailors to us. Accessing the magic is now easier than when MG did it. Explorers can make their own way how they please, by sailboat or motorboat, by trailer sailer or rib, launched at a strategic point anywhere along the way – or by road.

Because, rest assured, you don't need a boat at all to be able to enjoy the Swatchways. They are definitely for everybody. Their magic is in the creeks, the banks, the nature and the sounds of the local wildlife and many of the best places can be reached by car and still take in the views, the local scene or a decent pub.

To get there, be there and enjoy the magic is the aim. Carpe diem. Still magical after all these years.

The road to the Ramsholt Arms

"Where be the magical Swatchways, then?"

Many people who have read MG's book, or have at least heard of the Swatchways, even those living around East Anglia and the Essex/Suffolk coast, ask this question. Yet MG knew and knew what they meant in 1932.

We knew it, too, 50 years ago. 'The Swatchways' was a well used term by the good old sailor boys of the East Coast who mentored us as kids. What they said and what MG created as the title for his book coincide. They provide the definition of a coastal sea area made up of the rivers and creeks that abound between Foulness Island and the River Crouch to the southward and Aldeburgh to the north, embracing the Crouch and Roach, Blackwater, Colne, Mersea Quarters, the Stour, Orwell, Ore and the Alde, penetrating to the very limits of their high-tide navigability.

Along the way are many little bays or creeks to explore and anchor in peace and quiet and many a place to stop for a run ashore – or, nowadays, to rest in a marina that seems to nestle right into the marshes thereabouts. Tidal, but that's what opens up the upper reaches and provides a good percentage of the motive power to get there or back again.

Muddy at low tide but with a fair spattering of sandy beaches. Birds and seals abound. Fish to be caught from the sea. Cockpit cocktails, supper on board...or launch the dinghy and head for the light glow of a friendly pub ashore. On at least one of our stops, the village curry house was only a minute or two away from a deep-water mooring basin! MG may not have approved – or would he?

The Swatchways are not secret. They are accessible, beautiful, still there to be shared after all these years and still magical.

CHARLES SCOONES TRAVELS FROM THE OTHER SIDE OF THE WORLD

The clear deep waters of New Zealand are probably as different and as far away as it is possible to go from the Swatchways – the Hauraki Gulf has been my sailing playground for the past 30 years. But it was a sudden deluge of rain unique to Auckland that chased me into an antiquarian bookshop one day and, drifting into the maritime section, I came across an old copy of 'The Magic of the Swatchways'. The rain had long stopped and the sun was steaming the footpath by the time I emerged with the book in my hand.

I was weaned on the same creeks and East Coast rivers that Maurice Griffiths describes so well. I soon found the chapter in which he took his first sail on the little barge yacht 'Swan'. The words brought back strong memories for me as, not long before moving to New Zealand and newly married, I had been the proud owners of 'Swan'. In the years since, I often wondered what had become of her...by now she would be over a

A classic day in Auckland Harbour

century old, if indeed still afloat. It was not long before a twist of fate was to provide me with the answer.

In recent years I have been drawn back to England regularly, spending the summer months exploring the inland waterways by narrowboat and then escaping back to the Antipodes when the days grow short and the leaves turn brown and crunchy.

Inevitably, during these sojourns in the old country, sailing mates from way back would drag me without too much resistance for a pint or two in some of our old East Coast haunts.

It was in the Ship Inn at Levington that I had one of those 'I've been here before' feelings, as I ducked below a blackened beam, and then again in Maldon when, down a narrow street, I glimpsed for a second a row of barge topsails.

I found that the magic was still there, standing on the Hythe at Maldon, running my eyes over the same restored sailing barges alongside with their unique smell of tar, linseed, and tanned canvas. There was the chuckle of the ebbing tide around the huge rudders and

Topsail barges on Maldon quay

Falmouth Quay Punts would stand out into the channel to meet inbound ships (watercolour by Archie White)

leeboards. How would it feel to revisit these waters, I wondered, or had it all changed?

My childhood memories were of car journeys down the Southend Arterial road to Burnham-on-Crouch on a Friday evening, wedged in the back seat with smelly tanned canvas sails and coils of hemp rope. My weekend world was the fo'c'sle of our family yacht 'Bonita'. A converted Falmouth Quay Punt, she was a deep-draft, gaff-rigged yawl, more suited to the Cornish coast than the shallows of East Anglia.

I learned by a kind of salty osmosis from my father how he worked the tides, the tell-tale look of the water over mud or sand, how the new flood crept up against the last of the ebb along the shallow edges of the river, about the seasonal equinox tides when we eased into the mud berth for the winter and how to lay on coats of varnish in the few dry springtime hours.

During the family summer cruising, I would be gone for hours in the dinghy, rowing up imaginary Amazon rivers and often leaving mum and dad stranded ashore

I sailed many miles in 'Jacandor'

or, worse still, aboard, till beyond the pub closing time.

Dad eventually resolved the issue by buying me a boat of my own, 'Jacandor', a rugged little 14ft clinker dinghy.

With a boom tent, primus stove and a little Seagull outboard, I explored the length of the Crouch and Roach rivers. Mates would come along at weekends and we eventually explored far beyond Shore Ends. I think that little boat helped me later through the dangerous teenage years.

Back then, Maurice Griffiths was a name I knew as something to do with 'Yachting Monthly' magazine. I don't think I read much about the Swatchways. We just cast off with soggy paper charts in plastic folders and let the winds and tides be our tutors. Along the way, we would rub shoulders with the old salts in the pubs and, for the price of a pint, we learned when to take the tide over the Rays'n (Ray Sand Channel) and when not to and where to find a 'lee'. We listened to yarns about the sailormen, smugglers and privateers. We slowly became 'East Coasters'.

All the while that I was sailing out of Burnham, Paul Antrobus was sailing from Brightlingsea, also in Essex. Our sailing careers eventually crossed as crew aboard a grand old Fife racing yacht 'Evenlode' and, although we probably didn't appreciate it at the time, it is clear that we shared a fascination for the Swatchways.

Wind the clock forward to recent times when Paul was staying with us in Auckland. The America's Cup was still in New Zealand hands. Paul was browsing through my copy of Griffiths' book. "You know," he said, "the magic is still there. You can still do all that."

"OK," says I. "Maybe it's time to revisit the Swatchways!"

The tranquil Swatchways await

CHAPTER 1

Barging down to the Swatchways

St Katharine Docks to Maldon

Once a busy commercial dock in the Port of London, St Katharine Docks is now a vibrant marina just a heaving line's throw downstream of Tower Bridge. Not the Swatchways by any stretch of the imagination but important nonetheless as it is directly accessible from them up the 'London River', as Swatchways sailors call the Thames.

For many East Coasters, St Katharine Docks is the limit of navigation for a passage up the river. For us, it is a perfect starting point to set off downstream to the Thames Estuary and to head north beyond Harwich, in search of the old Swatchways magic.

Entry lock to St Katharine Docks...

...and the exit – to the river and thence the Swatchways

One day we were there, the rally for the Association of Thames Yacht Clubs had just ended but their spaces were quickly being taken by new entrants through the sea lock – sailing yachts, motorboats and the Harwich-registered Thames sailing barge 'Adieu', joining quite a number of similar Thames barges already resident there.

The river here is tidal but the dock, by definition, is not so vessels have to lock in and out, mainly at above half-tide level. With the bridge over the dock raised, spectators ashore get great entertainment from watching the boats going in or out.

A Thames barge leaving that way stirs the imagination even further. Today I am privileged to be aboard SB 'Phoenician', built in 1922, and you really feel you are off on a great trading voyage again, not just for a jolly around to Maldon.

We manoeuvre our vessel towards the lock and, as the footbridge across the entrance is raised, a small crowd gathers to watch us squeeze in.

As a Thames barge, we have traditional style, a tall

mast and top-mast and crew in slightly dirty jumpers, apparently de rigueur on a barge, and industrial Caterpillar boots. We look like seafarers from a bygone age all right. No yachting shoes, whites or captain caps here.

Years ago, a friend of mine, a crew on the shiny white, classic racing yacht 'Evenlode', managed to get an invitation to sail in a Thames barge match (bargees don't call them 'races'). He was very cocky about it and set off to the Butt & Oyster, Pin Mill, to join up with the rest of the crew, complete with reefer jacket, old but still smart ex-Navy holdall and his peak cap set at a jaunty angle. Into the pub he pranced, but his sartorial elegance was met by disdainful derision. He never did get aboard!

Perched high in the St Katherine's lock in our suitably theatrical and work-stained garb, it is easy to picture the old days of the trading square riggers coming in and out here. And we imagine the onlookers, so close and interested in us today, as relatives turned out in their finest to wish us 'God speed and a safe return!'

The lock begins to empty and we are gently lowered to the river, not far as we are leaving at top tide to turn

The holding quay for St Katharine's by Tower Bridge

to port to take the ebb and head downstream.

Our destination is Maldon. At the effective limit of upstream navigation of the River Blackwater, it's an ancient waterfront town just a jog away from Tollesbury and Heybridge Basin, haunts well documented in MG's narratives. Of course, you can go visit by road. But the only real way to go is to arrive aboard a Thames barge.

The passage from St Katherine Docks is a delivery trip to get repairs for ours following a prang in a barge match. These vessels are made of huge 10in by 6in planking but a T-bone collision, even at only three or four knots, can still do damage and the sheer size of the timbers means specialist skills are required to mend 'em. Those skills reside in Maldon.

In barge matches, although the sailing rules of the road are perfectly well known, there is also the "we Essex men never give way to a Kentish man" issue. It may all happen in slow motion but these matches are fiercely contested. Ask the Essex skipper why this is their way and he will say, "'Cos the Kentish will never give way to an Essex!"

There is no wind so we are motoring. These days, Thames barges have engines but they race as sail ships so only a small auxiliary engine is fitted. Ours gives us a maximum five knots through the water, barely enough to stem the current, so these big 90ft-plus stately ladies still have to work the tides to get where they want to.

We pass the lock to Limehouse Basin on our port side. Here there is a marina, the Cruising Association clubhouse and entry to Regent's Canal and the Limehouse Cut. Both link to Paddington Basin to connect with the Grand Union Canal or continue to rejoin the Thames upstream at Brentford lock. (The route is popular with narrowboats to avoid most of the tidal hazards of the Thames and get back to the river, heading for Oxford to rejoin the central canal system from there. A wonderful waterway for another day…)

Some of the most popular East End riverside pubs were once warehouses and private quays for barges in the 17th century. We pass by the Grapes at Limehouse and the Prospect of Whitby at Wapping, named after the barge 'Prospect ' which regularly plied from Whitby, North Yorkshire, to London to unload there. The pub is now a famous tourist attraction with good ales, a classy restaurant and fine river views. But the 'Prospect' herself and the wharf as a working wharf are long gone and sadly there is no way to moor alongside, even if the tide is up.

This part of the river is lined on both sides with little sandy beaches where East Enders of years ago used to bathe and harvest wild oysters for free.

Then the river's 'newest' hazard comes into view, the amazing Thames Barrier at Woolwich. It was built to prevent London flooding in the event of a very high tide

Approaching the Thames Barrier at Woolwich

coming upstream from the east and meeting excessive rainfall water coming down the length of the river from inland and the west.

Since opening in 1982, it has been used in anger 78 times for tide surge and 41 times for rain flood. There are scheduled monthly servicing closures, usually for three hours, so passage-making needs checking. Some say the flood risk has been enhanced by global warming, others that Britain is slowly tilting in the earth's crust so that London is more or less 'sinking' while Scotland rises.

On our passage we have to call up Barrier Control on the VHF to seek passage permission. We pass gracefully through gap number three, slightly disappointed to be motoring, not under sail, but no doubt more prudent. A modern motor barge, the 'Nigel Prior', is on her way upstream with building sand from Fingeringhoe, a Swatchways village up the river Colne, just short of Wivenhoe. We will visit there and see more of the Prior barges later.

Below the Barrier, the Thames, so pretty upstream at Henley and Marlow, becomes bleak and industrial in stark contrast. Luckily, dusk is beginning to fall and the ebb is about to end, so in traditional style we run ourselves gently on to the mud on the south side around Thames Mead/ Shadwell, dropping the hook into it with enough chain paid out for the expected 14ft rise to the next high tide. That is when, six hours later, we

The 'Nigel Prior' heads upstream through the Thames Barrier

will set off again with the ebb. Six hours off now for a beer, some supper and a short sleep.

The ship lifts and gently rocks us in slumber. Then we sense the barge turning to the new ebb and we all turn-to to weigh the anchor, hauled up slowly with the original pole-worked windlass. Hard work, but traditional. Luckily, the newer boat on which we shall explore the Swatchways later has a neat electric-power winch and this, we vote, is one of the 'good' elements of modern progress.

Still no wind, still dark, so on goes the little engine again.

We cross now to the Essex bank and scrape by Southend Pier. Less industrial now but still quite a bleak open vista with few contours. Another J J Prior motor barge passes us, also taking the ebb tide downstream and well inshore so we guess heading for Fingringhoe via the Swin to Wallet Spitway. Our plan is the same, but at a slower pace, to hit the Swin at low tide and then turn to port again, back on ourselves to take the flood up the Blackwater to Maldon.

Daylight now, sizzling bargee's full breakfast tucked away and the next landmark is the entrance to the Havengore, the short cut to the Rivers Roach and Crouch. We will explore this another day when the withies of the ancient Broomway path are clearly visible.

The Essex bank recedes away with the channel now a mile offshore. From a distance, we follow the contour of the uncovering mud bank with a careful eye on our depth line, by way of the West and East Swin, swinging to port around the South Whitaker buoy and across the Whitaker Channel entry to the Crouch.

We reach the Swin Spitway buoy and, as we go through

the channel towards the Wallet Spitway, yet another Prior barge, fully laden, passes us in the other direction to take the flood back up the Thames.

These barges are flat-bottomed to make them shallow draft for getting to the very top of little creeks at high tide and for sitting on the mud as it ebbs, then flows, loading their cargo in the intervening 12 hours.

The Prior barges carry sand and gravel for construction. In the past, the cargo was often hay to feed the horses key then to London's transport system, drawing Hackney cab people carriers, hearses, carts, carriages, brewers drays (very vital) and suchlike. The horse droppings were then brought back to fertilise the crop-growing land. Perfect recycling and the pace of life and loading set by the tides in those days.

There is a breeze now and the tide is with us so we drop a leeboard and set the main and foresail for a gentle broad reach. With no keel, our leeboards are dropped on the lee side to give lateral resistance to the power of the sails that all sailing vessels need to convert wind power into forward motion.

We sail upstream past the now mothballed Bradwell Nuclear Power Station. Since first generating electricity in 1962, this is one building which hasn't lasted the passing of time or usefulness that barges have done and wasn't there at all when MG sailed this way.

The power station now stands as a permanent landmark to guide the sea traveller. But when its many glass windows pick up the dramatic hues of a typical East Coast sunset, the casual watcher can easily be forgiven for imagining that a UFO or some other extraterrestrial object has just landed!

In the River Blackwater now, we leave Osea Island and

Maldon Hythe quay

the entrance to West Mersea to starboard and a couple of bends further up, hey presto, there are the small boat moorings and the charming houses and Jolly Sailor pub on the Maldon shore. With Thames barges already stacked side by side on the quay, quite a crowded scene greets us as it comes into view.

The river here is narrow, confined by the quay and the vessels to port but to starboard it is just marshes and river bank mini inlets. We brail up the mainsail and carry our 50 tons of way with the now gentle tide until halfway along the jetty, then luff up to starboard and plant our bow firmly into the marshes. The tide, still flowing upstream ever so slowly, takes our stern and this stately 90ft giant just turns in her own length. As we come nearly straight across the river, we back the jib, the bow falls off the marsh bank and swings off through the direction of the tide so that we gently crab across the stream towards the barge we are to moor alongside, already on the quay.

Well, that is how it is meant to be done! The skipper does actually have the little iron mate in tick-over and

The Jolly Sailor, Maldon

after we drop the jib he gives her a tiny nudge ahead, making sure we are properly lined up with the boat inside us. Then finish the brailing for a harbour stow. The young trainee mate is supposed to do this, climbing up the ratlines and tying in the ropes around the top sail and the high gaff. But ours is scared of heights so the skipper demonstrates for us. Wrap the sheets round the staysail in a fancy fashion so it hangs like a small sausage clear of the deck – that's the correct way to do the job.

Prominent on the quay is a red-painted old sea mine, converted to a collecting box. There are many such mines in the small ports of the Swatchways. This one is for the Shipwrecked Fishermen and Mariners' Royal Benevolent Society, founded 1939. The engraved message on it reads, 'There is sorrow on the sea.'

But not for us yet. Our barge passage is now over and it's time to let the crew get on with preparing for repairs. We are well into the Swatchways proper – and ready for more.

SAVED FOR THE NATION

St Katharine Docks has become home base to many historic Thames barges and to other smart sail and motor yachts on a semi-permanent basis. Some barges just moor up, some offer on-board entertaining without leaving the dock, some do the same with a short river trip included. But most are just waiting for the next barge match date, sitting out the winter and smartening up what little varnish work there is.

Fifty years or so ago, London very nearly lost St Katharine's altogether. With the migration of large shipping docks further east, it fell into disuse as a commercial dock and developers (and probably some councillors) wanted to knock down the old warehouses, fill it all in and build over it.

At that time, the 60s, London had no city-based marinas for private sailing yachts, nothing to match the dock at the Royal Maas Yacht Club, Rotterdam, where most of the fleet in the annual Harwich to Hook of Holland sailing race headed. It was a tragedy, a travesty

St Katharine's – home base for many Thames barges

even, that London had nothing similar. Luckily, the opportunity was spotted in the nick of time, articles appeared in papers and 'Yachts & Yachting' magazine and the dock was 'saved for the nation'.

St. Katharine's, in the heart of London's financial district, has developed into a thriving marina the size of eight football pitches. It is a huge asset to the capital, a pleasure for boaters arriving from the Thames upstream or those coming from the east coast or Holland, France, Germany and Belgium.

It also provides a delightful tourist walk, with the Tower of London and Tower Bridge right next door and a large hotel overlooking it all. The historic buildings in the dock have names that recall the trade that used to go on there, like Marble Quay and Ivory House. Many people live in flats in the converted warehouses, too. There are restaurants, shops and offices and a good pint to be had from a selection of real ales and international lagers in the Dickens Inn, plus a decent pub menu to feed off.

Thank goodness the campaign succeeded. Heritage once lost can never be regained.

The MV 'Havengore' is based there. A former Port of London Authority vessel, it's famous for transporting Winston Churchill's coffin along the Thames from Tower Pier to Festival Pier for the train journey from Waterloo to Bladon, Oxfordshire, for the private burial of the great man.

MV 'Havengore'

Among very ship-like

houseboats in the inner dock is the 100ft 'Flamant Rose', once owned by French legend Edith Piaf. Still luxuriously furnished in Parisian style, complete with gold plated bath and cream leather upholstery, the 'Little Sparrow's' film-set style yacht was, they say, her special place for secret trysts with her lover.

CHAPTER 2

Giraffes on the horizon!

From Maldon to Walton Backwaters and Ipswich Dock

For this trip, I set off from Liverpool Street Station, London, destination Maldon. MG did the same 70 years ago to join a seven ton yawl lying in Colliers Reach, walking the final couple of miles from Maldon East station. In his day the train went all the way to Maldon. Now you get off at Chelmsford and take the bus.

The train journey to Chelmsford is straightforward and rapid and the bus station is just across the road from the railway station. But the bus is only hourly and I have time to kill. Luckily, there is the pub, the Original Plough, a pleasant bar with front windows overlooking the bus stands. A nice pint of Doom Bar, some way from its Cornwall brewery (Sharp's at Rock) is taken on board while keeping a good look-out for any bus movement.

My bus will be at 1700 and I'd better catch it as there is only one more this evening. I do. The driver on what is a repetitive route, Chelmsford, Maldon, Burnham-on-Crouch, doesn't know of the quay at Maldon (official name Hythe Quay) so can't tell me the nearest stop to get off. I really want to know as it is tipping it down now and I do not have full oilskins with me, just a light sailing top for the June weather.

Another passenger tries to help but I can't catch what he says through his broad Essex brogue. So I just peer out of the rain-swept window and try to recognise a landmark or two from an earlier visit to the town. For information, the nearest stop is the Warwick Arms, another pub which seems to be something of a youngsters' night venue these days.

But, in my ignorance and not wishing to turn right and find myself on the town by-pass again en route for Burnham, I get off one stop too early. Not a big deal, except for the heavy rain which comes as squalls, so frequent short stops under shop awnings are necessary.

Eventually, down the steep hill and past the church, I see the masts and top rigging of Thames barges beckoning and, by them, the Jolly Sailor pub. Resisting it, I go on to the quay to find Charles with his 'Antiope' moored on the floating visitors' jetty, just upstream from the rafted-up sailing barges and, at this state of the tide, not floating at all.

'Antiope' is a 46ft steel, twin-engined, motor cruiser, chunky and go-anywhere business-like. What? Not a

'Antiope' on the visitor pontoon at Maldon Hythe Quay

sailing boat? I can tell you, I am drenched by now and she seems a pretty sensible mode of transport.

Sailing on the Swatchways is different from the pleasure of sailing on any other stretch of water because of their unique features, the remote anchorages to be found and their shoreside delights, if you want them. Probably best under sail rather than by motorboat but not for us this particular day, with the weather as it is.

The tide is flooding but the visitor berth still keeps us aground. We repair to the Queens Head as the nearest place to get out of the rain, to dry out outside and refresh inside. The windows give us a great view of the charter barges coming home up the River Blackwater, with somewhat damp-looking passengers attempting to get back to their berths sooner rather than later, although the water level is still a bit too low. With a squeeze, an engine push and a pull on a line already thrown ashore, they flat-bottom across the mud and make it.

Maldon is blessed with two well known pubs on the waterside. The Jolly Sailor is the pretty one, attracting tourists and photographers alike, 17th century quaint, with a good view of the quay and a nice range of beers and pub food. To the left, downstream of the Jolly Sailor, is the Maldon Little Ship Club clubhouse, open weekends. At the end of the quay, long-established specialist barge yard Cooks is well worth a peek. This particular day, a historic steam tug boat is in the process of renovation on the jetty.

The second pub, the Queens Head. at the up-river end and right on the quay, is deceptively plain to look at from the outside but full of character and colour inside. Big windows and a spacious terrace of tables overlook the berths containing an interesting array of boats,

Hythe Quay

some of them classics. It has a nice bar and a decent food menu. The rear bar, which would have been the public bar in the old days, is the usual haunt of the working bargemen and local shipyard craftsmen. They don't need views of the water for relaxation but this is where to go to glean the yarns, the folklore and local knowledge straight from the mouths of these experienced and gentlemanly people.

We stay in the waterfront bar watching the action until, as the tide rises, the rain stops and the sky starts to brighten. Time for supper on board. We are not leaving from our floating jetty until tomorrow's morning tide.

We have a cosy supper in the cabin and next morning are floating sufficiently by 1030 to get off the dock. The sailing barges are already afloat and leaving.

It becomes second nature to East Coast sailors to 'take the tide' to wherever. Once off the quay and looking back from the water, Maldon looks much the same as we remembered it from years before. Maybe more Thames barges alongside now but it is probably little different from the time when Maurice Griffiths sailed from here.

The Byrhtnoth

We head down the Blackwater following the barge 'Thistle' which has embarked a crowd of about 30 school kids festooned in matching pirate bandana hats. And, underlining our point that these Swatchways are for all kinds, a canal narrowboat slips by, heading upstream to take our place on the visitor pontoon.

We snake around the meandering river, with Maldon Yacht Club and the bronze statue of Byrhtnoth to starboard. Byrhtnoth was an 'Earldorman' of Essex who led the English forces against a Viking invasion at the Battle of Maldon in 991. The Anglo-Saxons fought heroically but eventually were totally beaten.

Soon we are off the entrance to Heybridge Basin. This pretty little village in Colliers Reach, the name of the Blackwater at this point, is on the sea lock to the canalised River Chelmer, whence the town of Chelmsford gets its name.

A small keelboat can stay afloat in Colliers Reach at least until half tide. Once through the lock, Heybridge Basin is a favourite place for laying-up. Among its many attractions, it has two good pubs, the Jolly Sailor (yes, another one) and the Old Ship, a tearoom and a shellfish café.

The Old Ship is in a sunny aspect, with tables outside and a fine view of activities in the lock – and serving

Heybridge Basin

Adnams (of Southwold) and Greene King (of Bury St Edmunds) beers and the usual selection of lagers and wines. The Jolly Sailor, down below the sea wall, is a good fun pub featuring local Maldon Gold Summer Ale, Old Speckled Hen and other guest ales. Both offer a pub food menu.

For visitors coming by river, there is a small floating dinghy pontoon below the sea wall. By car, there is a certain amount of pub parking but this is a popular spot on a sunny weekend so can get very full. Arriving

Colliers Reach

by water is highly recommended.

The canal, officially the Chelmer and Blackwater Navigation, is 13 miles and 12 locks up to Chelmsford through charming Essex countryside, with a towpath to walk it or boats to hire if you fancy a short trip. The first stretch of waterway contains a fascinating, eclectic collection of craft of all types, each with its own tale to tell but many seemingly long-term laid up or awaiting restoration, minor or major.

In 1860, a rail link to London's Liverpool Street Station to Maldon was built but closed down in 1966. MG had used it to get to Colliers Reach, walking from Maldon East Station to Heybridge. That's how it was done at that time. Down to the coast on the Friday evening train, a weekend of sailing, then back on a Sunday train from wherever you had got to. There was even a special yachtsman's ticket to do it in those days. In many ways it was a simpler life back then, with boats, trains and far fewer cars. But it can still be done if we are minded to.

We follow the channel buoys, quite narrow at times near the top of Osea Island with its fine white turreted house. Then Maylandsea and the Blackwater Sailing Club. We are heading downstream to Mersea or Bradwell

The Green Man, Bradwell Creek

for the night or perhaps, if conditions suit, to continue on up the coast to the Walton Backwaters. Part of the magic of sailing the East Coast is there is usually an anchorage close by at the turn of the tide.

Bradwell Creek now has an all-tide marina, a big plus compared with the muddy hard of old. Just up the hill from the jetty and boatyard is the Green Man, a friendly pub with local brewery beers on the pumps. In the bar, there is an ancient cryptic sign that has been there at least 40 years to our knowledge and has thankfully been preserved by successive landlords. It can be read as a sentence if you can discover the cipher (no prizes offered for the solution).

Charles recalls how he had moored his barge yacht 'Swan' in Bradwell Creek for a season and how in the sailing club down by the old hard he had discovered his father's name, Arthur Scoones, on the honours board among its founders.

The weekend atmosphere and activity is comfortingly little changed. The quay and moorings in the channel look just as they were then but, of course, now there is a new cut through the old seawall giving entry to the well appointed and well disguised marina.

Modern 'advances' since 1932 may be derided by purist sailors but not by us. We think marinas, as a case in point, make the Swatchways' magic more accessible and more enjoyable, especially for going there as a family.

Marinas were not available back then and as they developed they were often strongly resisted by locals, even the local yachtsmen. The reasons they gave mainly were that marinas spoilt the scenery and made swing moorings obsolete so the river would have no boats on it to look at! But probably the real reason was simply resistance to change. The UK was years behind continental Europe in this respect but finally marinas arrived and were gradually accepted.

Here in the Swatchways on our revisit we find their presence hardly noticeable. They are well landscaped into the river banks and only the cluster of masts above the sea walls are a visual clue to their existence. They are pretty full, but so are all the swing moorings out in the rivers. They are clearly providing many more places to keep a boat (even MG himself had to agree to this when he was editor of 'Yachting Monthly', we found out later in our trip) while the magical substance of the Swatchways remains unaffected.

For the family cruiser, marinas offer perhaps the only way to explore these waters harmoniously. Use their facilities to start and finish each day, supper ashore in a

Well landscaped Tollesbury marina

good pub, walk the ship's dog and make the task a whole lot easier. MG used to wade the mud to get to his craft. Why add such hardship to the trip when nowadays there's no need to?

Marina sailors can arrive when no-one else is around, leap aboard, get an early night, set off at first light in peace and quiet and find a creek for an overnight anchorage, as we did up the Roach on another voyage. Light evenings, the tantalising smell of the boat barbecue, then back to base next day. Hop off, leave the boat safely, return home for work and schools on Monday at the end of a weekend that was magical for all.

Having paid our respects to Bradwell Creek and the tide still with us, on we go again. The squat blocks of Bradwell Nuclear Power Station look threatening and sinister today with no sun on the windows. The estuary now widens with Mersea Island and the Colne to Brightlingsea opening up to port. This time we will bypass the Colne at the Bench Head buoy, heading north with the tide towards Harwich.

On the port side we pass the east cardinal post that

marks the Molliette wreck, covered now and sunk into the mud even at low tide.

When we were kids, this wreck still showed above the waves and its green wreck buoy was one of the racing marks for the Brightlingsea dinghy racing fleet. At our tender age it was a significant challenge as it was nearly out of sight from the sailing club starting box. With zero provision of rescue boats in those days, it felt like an offshore passage to us teenagers as we rounded it in its relatively exposed coastal position. Could this have been sowing the seeds for our future love of offshore racing and cruising, we wonder to each other.

The Molliette is a favourite spot for local fishermen and sea anglers and as we sail by there is already a boat with two rods out. Such peace and contentment they get – and sometimes supper!

The Inner Bench Head and Colne Point buoys all slip by as we head up close to the Colne Point shore, looking for some shelter from the westerly which has kicked up a chop in the more open water here.

The Inner Bench Head flashes two red every 10 seconds. This Trinity House buoy is powered by solar panels and a generator driven by wave motion. In 'them days' the fishermen and Brightlingsea rowing boat ferrymen that we kids looked up to called it "the gas light". No-one now at Trinity House can tell us why and no-one says it was ever powered by gas. So it remains a mystery of folklore for ever. But it's still an important turning mark for the two rivers in the Colne/Blackwater estuary – and the Swin passage to the Crouch and Burnham and to the Thames – and for us for the inside passage up the coast to Harwich, our immediate target. A buoy not to be trifled with, we give it a respectful nod and take a picture for the record.

Crossing the Colne, the Force 4 westerly has built up a chop and 'Antiope' is rolling. We have both sailed thousands of offshore and ocean miles. We are used to sailing in swells with yachts with a keel and sails to press us to leeward, but at the same time dampening the motion, and quite accustomed to steering or sitting down low and close to the water as it rushes by or splashes into the cockpit. This experience on 'Antiope' is quite different and new to both of us.

We are dry and high above the water about two metres at aft deck level, four at eye level, with less than one metre of draught below the waterline. Good news for later in the shallow Swatchways but sparse for the current chop off Colne Point.

The upper deck steering position is covered by a substantial canvas hood considerably more enclosed than the usual spray dodger that most cruising yachts run to. We proceed at a leisurely and fuel-efficient rate, making about seven knots which is comparable with the speed a sail boat would be doing reaching in this weight of wind. And we roll several degrees each side.

A sailing yacht heels and rocks a bit but generally stays heeled on one side or the other. The motor yacht, having no steadying influence from a sail, rolls to both sides and sometimes performs two or three sudden quite violent staccato rolls in a row. The roll is no more than 10 degrees.

A yacht may well be sailing at a steady 10 to 15 degrees of heel, with more in the gusts. We are quite used to that and it usually feels good and exhilarating. On the motor yacht it feels like a bigger angle (it's not) without a regular rhythm or the predictable motion that you get on the sail boat. High on the upper bridge deck, the rolling seems unnatural and pronounced.

The teak deck furniture starts to slide about unnervingly and bits of rope to tie it all in place are rapidly deployed. But down below in the deck saloon, or a few more steps down into the galley and dining area at more or less waterline level, the roll is hardly felt at all. A good place for queasy people to gather in the warm and watch the passing scenery on the shore through the portholes.

With time, we get our sea legs and learn how to feel the boat and the seas working together. You have to hang on to something or wedge in, but so you do on a sail yacht. It's just a different set of sea legs required. And down in the galley it is no trouble at all to brew up a couple of coffees.

The tide is swooshing us onwards north-east and we begin to get sea shelter from Colne Point and the Priory Spit.

The passage up to Harwich is relatively featureless. The coastline is very level and bland, brightened only by traditional beach huts immaculately painted, much photographed and often featured in glossy colour supplements in the fashionable spirit of nostalgia that has grown so popular. There is even an annual web-based Beach Hut of the Year competition!

Clacton's famous pier sticks out proud from the level shoreline, its new 50ft high, red and white, helter-skelter tower now a very prominent focal point.

Years ago, when we were racing on the EAORA (East Anglian Offshore Racing Association) circuit, we sailed out here to round the Radio Caroline pirate radio station ship on an 'Evenlode' crew training trip. She

'Evenlode' in the 60s

was a classic Fife double-ender with the metre yacht characteristics Fife was famous for. Then owned by Bertie Hall and sailed under the Royal Corinthian Yacht Club (Burnham) burgee, she was already a 50-year-old classic, built originally for Colin Ratsey of Ratsey & Lapthorne sail-making fame in Cowes on the Isle of Wight.

A fast race winner in her day, 'Evenlode' was hopeless under the new rating rules then emerging. We were often scratch boat and came home first and very occasionally actually won on handicap, if the tide turned against the rest of the fleet just as we were crossing the line and finishing. This happened once luckily for us at Southend Town Regatta and we won the Southend Golden Rose Bowl trophy, thrilling the owner's wife to bits. Needless to say, the champagne flowed at the ensuing highly celebratory crew party.

We had sailed out and rounded the Radio Caroline as a test windward mark as it was of a similar size to lightships like the Cork and Sunk that were often on EAORA courses. We had the station tuned in and waved madly, in the hope they would play us a request. We couldn't phone – mobiles hadn't been invented back in the 1960s, of course – and the Caroline crew couldn't understand our semaphore either. But they played a record "for the nice white yacht sailing round us" anyway! Then we were away, back to Burnham.

Modern-day Swatchways sailors may well be too young to remember the several pirate radio ships which were off Harwich, but we oldies still remember the songs and sing them! They certainly brought about radical change to the UK radio scene, most would say for the better. The Richard Curtis 2009 film 'The Boat that Rocked' is a lighthearted comedy set in 1966 but does tell roughly the story of how it all happened when the 'pirates' won against the British government.

This time we plough on towards Harwich, gazing at Frinton's smart new blocks of sea-view flats which contrast dramatically with the Victorian splendour of the old Grand Hotel, converted recently into yet more up-market residences. Our destination is amended from Harwich to the Walton Backwaters. We pass Walton Pier, keeping quite far offshore as it is now low tide and the mud flats come out from the shore some distance hereabouts.

We squeeze into Nelson's famous Medusa Channel, the Naze Tower alerts us and excitement builds as we keep our eyes peeled to spot the Pye End buoy. You can't turn into the Backwaters channel until the Pye End is reached. Actually, there is a cut through we heard about later but you need to be a local for it to be a viable passage. The sand banks are hidden by the water. It all looks navigable but below are concealed, twisting rivers.

The 'giraffes' of Felixstowe

We spot the red and white Pye End buoy. Behind it, the conspicuous cranes at Felixstowe Docks look like a row of striding giraffes to us. We sail right up to the buoy to make sure – it is low water now with the flood just beginning – and take photographs for good measure. Sharp hairpin turn to port and we creep up the well buoyed channel of Hamford Water, but watching carefully on the chart plotter as we go. How MG would have loved – I am sure not rejected or abhorred – this electronic masterpiece that adds so much to the safety, certainty and therefore the pleasure of modern-day cruising.

Pye End buoy

This is a real hidden river in a wide expanse of flat water. The buoys are sponsored by local firms or sailing clubs and need to be followed closely. We head back south-west now and into the wind. Very soon the seaway has disappeared and we progress in flat water, with hard sand now beginning to wrap around us. We reckon cricket could be played on these sands at low tide, just as they do on the Brambles Bank in the Solent. There it is only once year at the lowest autumn tide for about an hour. Here, we muse, it could be on every low tide.

Old lighters are laid sunken along the inner marshes to protect the banks from erosion. Then we come to the moorings in Walton Channel through the most amazing chicane of buoys. It is low water so we turn back after a while into Hamford Water and up into Landermere Creek. Slowly. The mud is soft here and it takes us several seconds to notice when we are no longer actually moving, just gently aground. No retreat.

We wait for the tide to eventually lift us and head back to set the anchor for the night in Kirby Creek, one of Walton Backwaters' most enchanting anchorages. One or two other boats there but otherwise totally quiet. The absolute magic that we came for. Perfect sundowners on the after deck, with the deck furniture now in place again in a neat, friendly circle. Ginger-coloured seals on the banks stare across at us and occasionally slide into the water to swim over for a closer look.

The water just ripples now as our shallow draught comes into its own. Smells of supper on the way waft up from below, making us think about MG. How often his stories ended with the pleasure of the sound and smell of "sizzling on the stove below", seemingly the redeeming moment of many of his passages. Not for us in quite the same way, with our sundowner cocktails and acres of space on the upper deck, but just as welcome after our passage made, complete with its new rolling sea experiences. So we tuck in and talk about the Swatchways until the darkness and the dinner wine send us to our bunks.

Next day we set off for Ipswich. We shall return to the Backwaters later to really explore its innermost nooks and creeks in a smaller boat and the illustrious company of the local Warden.

Lifting anchor at 0830, the stillness is everywhere. A yacht passes us on a gentle broad reach down Hamford Water, under the watchful eyes of the ginger seals. She looks so good that, just for a moment, we wish we were back on a sail boat ourselves. The yacht turns up into Walton Creek. We head on back to Pye End buoy, easier to find this time, and on a gently rising tide head towards the striding giraffes of Felixstowe.

Leaving the docks to starboard and Harwich to port, we enter the Orwell. Calm water now with rolling grassy banks and woodland, in soft contrast to the flatness of the Clacton to Walton-on-the-Naze coastline a few miles away.

The hard at Pin Mill and the Butt & Oyster

We press on, yacht moorings begin to appear and then we are off Pin Mill. So peaceful, so photogenic and the Butt & Oyster pub beckoning. The tide goes out a long way here so mooring off and launching the dinghy is the only way ashore. But there is a firm hard from low water to high, which is why the sailing barges liked it so much as a base.

Harry King and Sons' traditional boat yard still operates, building sailing boats and dinghies and offering fitting out and any other work, as it has done for over a century and a half. Two boats for 'Swallows and Amazons' author Arthur Ransome were built here.

Spring launching is done by taking the yachts down the hard on trailers to nearly low-water mark, then waiting for the tide to come in. Hauling ashore for winter is achieved in the reverse manner. A substantial scrubbing posts and barge grids facility has been there for years but now there is electric power for power-hose washing and scrubbing. Progress!

From the hills above the water's edge hamlet, a small river tumbles down and wiggles around the top of the hard, eventually running out beside it to the sea – a miraculous natural phenomenon as it provides the landing facility for dinghies. The special technique for dragging a dinghy up this rill is to lead the painter back round a rowlock in the forward position and walk up the edge on the stony hard, pulling gently. The dinghy comes with you, parallel, not butting into the shore. (It's the same at West Mersea, too, and anywhere you need the dinghy to run parallel to your track instead of pulling in to jam on the bank.)

We work out where you need to be for the time ashore versus the tide's progress, fix the dinghy on a loose painter so others can pass if desired and then head for the Butt & Oyster.

This 17th century pub has original flagstones, an unchanged bar, a huge fireplace which is roaring in winter, free WiFi and excellent Adnams of Southwold draught beers. The bistro-style eatery serves all-day breakfast, a typical pub menu and specials such as fresh dressed crab at a price that doesn't break the bank.

You can walk a while along the foreshore to view the yachts and the work in progress at Harry King's. Go to the end and you'll find Pin Mill Sailing Club, only open weekends but visitors welcome.

This must be one of the most photographed and painted scenes in the whole of the Swatchways. "Speak of the Orwell, and every East Coast cruising man immediately sees a picture of Pin Mill," wrote famous East Coast cruising man Jack Coote in his book 'East Coast Rivers', my edition dated 1979. And surely it is still thus.

'East Coast Rivers' was originally published by 'Yachting Monthly'. It is now part of the Wiley Nautical 'Cruising Companion' series, a comprehensive pilot guide taking in all our Swatchways destinations. Go to www.eastcoastrivers.com for regular updates.

We get back aboard and head for Ipswich Haven Dock, now a very popular marina right in the heart of the town. On the way, we sail by undulating country and the occasional sailing club, then under the impressive Orwell Bridge. Opened in 1982, it carries A14 traffic towards Norfolk, bypassing Ipswich to great effect.

We pass by Fox's Marina to port and the busily working Ipswich docks to starboard. It's tidal up here so there's a lock for going into Haven Marina which is open at high tide. We just make it and sail straight in.

Ipswich Haven Marina

A couple of Thames sailing barges, 'Victor' and 'Hydrogen', regular competitors in barge matches, are lying against the town wharf beneath the imposing old Town Hall.

The marina is nearly full but some visitor berths are available and one is assigned to us over the VHF. After a false start to find it first time round, we squeeze into a berth hard against the inner quay at the top of the floating jetties. A little tricky but very handy for the office block and facilities, the Last Anchor café/bar and Ipswich Haven Yacht Club (visiting yachtsmen welcome).

This trip is done. 'Antiope' awaits new crew before crossing to Holland. For the rest of us, all that remains is to walk to the nearby station and, as MG would have done, get back to Liverpool Street by train. Magic over, at least for the time being!

CHAPTER 3

Neaped but not thirsty

The Deben to Ramsholt and Woodbridge and the Alde to Snape Maltings

Maurice would have frowned if he knew.

Sailing 'Swan' was a series of new experiences. We had made Benfleet our home-base back in the late 60s when the old Trinity House lightship was the yacht club clubhouse and during the winter months the pot belly stove would glow red in the bar.

Our little barge yacht could sneak home up the creek long after the tide deadline for keelboats. We often cruised in company with 'Growler', another little barge yacht. The daily schedule was dictated by finding sandy beaches for the kids and the occasional pub for the grown-ups. If we could arrange the two together, everyone was happy.

'Growler'

One such lucky combination was at Ramsholt on the River Deben. On this cruise our timing had been perfect: high tide, sand, sunshine and opening time. We literally sailed up the beach, 'Growler' and 'Swan' alongside each other, just a few dry-shod paces from the bar. In those days, we were unaware of 'day skipper' courses. We learned seamanship through experience. We were about to learn lesson one.

Of course we knew about the tidal changes but we were in holiday mode. From the terrace of the Ramsholt Arms, the sight of our brailed up sails and varnished spars gave us a feeling of pride. We extolled the virtues of shallow-draft barge yachts and tried to ignore the comments from the other sailors about this being the last of the springs and that a nice big high was moving in.

The morning tide washed around the hulls but they stayed firmly aground. We made a show of scrubbing a bit of weed off around the waterline every time someone came close by. We enjoyed the local hospitality again and built grand sandcastles. Over the next few days, we thoroughly explored the shoreline, became a popular subject for watercolour artists and resisted requests for ground rent. Stakes marked the daily receding tide lines.

Our summer cruise curtailed, we made plans to leave

Ramsholt Arms and beach

Ramsholt harbour master's office

the boats and return in a week's time. Then, a stroke of luck! The heat-wave ended, the pressure dropped and a gale from the east pushed more water into the Deben. In the middle of the night the boat stirred. In the dark, with the wind howling around us, we kedged ourselves down the beach. When the two barges returned to Benfleet, it took a while to live down the story once the kids had shopped us.

Today, that infamous beach is still outside the Ramsholt Arms. You still have to make a certain effort to get here, either by road or water, but once settled on the terrace or the grass there are few locations to beat it. Out in the anchorage a couple of Dutch ensigns fly. And the harbour master's unique waterside office alongside the old wharf is quite unmistakable in letterbox red.

Arriving from the sea, this delightful river demands some respect and care. Over the years I have crossed this bar several times. It was never routine, the leading marks were sometimes difficult to see in poor light and the bar buoy would seem to disappear into the troughs. Today, with the latest electronics aboard, the task can be easier but even the chart plotter should not be trusted as the sandbanks can change almost overnight. Although today's chart shows less than a metre at low tide over the bar, quite sizeable yachts have made the Deben their home. (The website www.eastcoastrivers.com provides regular chartlets and information.)

Ideally, your first bar crossing should be with a fair

tide, nearly full, and just a moderate breeze off the land. Only with experience should you try it below half-tide ebb or with an onshore wind. From the green outside the Ferryboat Inn at Felixstowe Ferry, you may see the bizarre sight of a tall sail gliding smoothly along just beyond the seawall, only to start bucking wildly as the yacht meets the waters over the bar.

For the sailor coming in from seaward, what a contrast to see dinghy sailors in the flat waters just beyond the narrows, and you have a chance now to relax and enjoy the scene. Bawdsey Manor dominates the north shore, showing no hint now of its importance during the last war. It was here that James Watson-Watt, a direct descendant of James Watt, perfected radar and the early warning system that had certainly helped the Allies win the Battle of Britain.

The hamlet of Felixstowe Ferry, to the south, hides behind the sea wall. The ferry landing, black fishermen's huts and a boatyard all crowd the point before the river widens and the current sweeps us on up river.

By the time we have turned a couple of bends, the open sea seems very distant as green hills and forests surround us. We sail past the Ramsholt Arms today, heading for a quiet night at Waldringfield, a row ashore and a pint in the Maybush. The cartoonist Giles obviously knew this pub well – his depictions of the Giles family boating are immortalised in the bar.

Maurice Griffiths would have been very familiar with the waters above Waldringfield. The twists and turns are challenging for anyone with a deep draft. But the reward is a visit to the charming old town of Woodbridge. Or a walk up the hill to Sutton Hoo and the site of the seventh century Anglo Saxon burial ship. Here there is now an

The Maybush at Waldringfield

all-tide marina and the trains still run. It was from the same rail station that Griffiths embarked on many of his voyages. But be prepared to leave on the same tide or dry out if there is no room in the marina.

Another day the voyage was the Alde to Snape Maltings.

"The Voice of the Shingle" was how MG described the coast north of Orford Haven in his vivid description of a voyage in 'Seamew', a six ton barge yacht of uncertain vintage. His tale of their desperate efforts to avoid being swept on to this shore in a rising gale and finally crossing the bar is the stuff of nightmares for a sailor.

I wanted to revisit this spot, having never been to the river mouth from the land before.

We arrive by road at the lonely settlement of Shingle Street. Little has changed. The white coastguard cottages that I remember from seaward still watch over the shifting banks. The sound of the stones being sucked and rearranged by the waves greet us as we open the car doors.

Climbing the bank, the scene before us is dramatic.

Shingle Street looking towards Orford Castle

The ebb tide is twisting out of the River Ore, finally making a break for the sea, and white water marks the bar far out beyond the humps of shingle. The river mouth has been pushed ever southwards over the centuries. A green channel marker leans to the current. The castle at Orford is just visible in the distance, built to guard a port that is now far from the sea.

I have navigated this entrance myself often enough when sailing 'Swan' and by dinghy and, unlike Griffiths, we had the benefit of an engine or at the least an outboard motor. Sitting now on the steep stony shore, a motor boat comes surging down the stream and out to sea, confidently finding the deepest water with the assistance, no doubt, of up-to-date instruments.

The following day, we have an invitation from a good friend, Robin Gibbon, to take the tide from Sloughden Quay, Aldeburgh, up to Snape Bridge in his 19ft Cornish Shrimper 'Emily Ann'. I was not going to miss an opportunity to revisit our mooring site just below the bridge.

Robin is a member of Aldeburgh Yacht Club and the launch runs us quickly out to the mooring. Despite the summer shower, all is dry below. I wonder if these craft would have suited MG or did he relish the hardship of a leaky boat? Dry down below with no chance of straining the timbers in a seaway, surely the Shrimper concept, shallow draft with centreboard, trailerable and with an easily handled gaff rig, would have met with his approval.

Once aboard the 'Emily Ann', our skipper sends us scurrying and in no time we have sail up, slip the mooring in a very gentle Force 2 and are soon around the first bend, out of sight of Aldeburgh. The club regatta fleet is working up the river with us, short tacking into the dying breeze being drawn off the land by the North Sea, but we are going further upstream beyond the last of the club's racing marks just by Barber's Reach.

The bay here widens but the underwater channel does not and the passage winds its way through withies marked by red bottles and green tapes. Stray out of line and you pay the price. Robin, we are to discover, has never before sailed upstream of Iken Cliff, even though he has been sailing this river for several years.

We press on into Church Reach by Iken Church. Then, with a sharp turn to port and heading almost south, we enter a very tricky passage with right-angle bends, all under water and all requiring a sharp look out to ensure the next withy is really the next and not just a trick of perspective. This bit is aptly named the Lower Trouble-some Reach.

Ahead there is another right-angle bend with a

Iken church – an important landmark

Thames barge moored at its apex, which encourages us that all is possible. This bend is called Troublesome Reach. Two tricky bits, one after the other. Sometimes the red and green top-knots on the withies are missing and you have to work out the likely geometry of the channel to decide which is next and which side to pass.

We have done well as far as Iken church and through the 'troublesome' reaches but then we get the logic of a missing top-knot wrong. The deep water is not on the side we thought and we come quietly and gracefully to a stop, the flooding tide now beginning to overtake us.

As we calculate how long we might take to float over the mudbank, a tripper boat swings around the bend upstream. It heads straight for us and passes us barely a boat's width away, a knowing smile on the face of the skipper. Then comes the admission from our host that this was new territory for him as well as us. His last yacht had been deep draft, making these waters out of bounds.

The tripper skipper's wide, flat-bottomed boat goes on down and round the bend to Iken Church Reach. We, having observed where he has left its wake, apply gib-backing and punting skills, using the old premise that the best way off a mudbank is back the way you got on. So we go astern and manage to refloat ourselves.

The tripper boat comes back and the pressure is on to sail the boat as fast as we can to be able to follow him up the river. He goes faster and we are again left to our own devices. But before we get to Snape he is back again with a second load of trippers, just in time to give us a hint for rounding the last two bends. Hardly any wind and with the clock ticking, we fire up the handy little inboard engine neatly tucked out of sight under the cockpit floor.

You have to get very close indeed under the port hand bank in very exaggerated fashion to make the last bend, almost able to touch the grassy towpath. Running the tripper boat, we reflect, is a rather quirky business with only a couple of hours a day when it's feasible to sell tickets. We think it might rather suit us some time in the future!

The distinctive roofline of Snape Maltings is by now tantalisingly close and we squeeze round the corner. There is the landing jetty for the tripper boat and then the quay stretching almost up to the bridge. It was built to get sailing barges right into the farming land, so typical of this part of the world, and in their day a vital opening of commerce and prosperity, now long since overtaken by road transport. What they carried was malted barley for brewing from the imposing brick and stone-built malting barns.

With the coming of road and rail, this charming little port became redundant and the maltings ceased in any case in 1965. And that would have been that, except composer Benjamin Britten declared that the acoustics of the deserted old buildings would make for a splendid concert hall. This was achieved in 1967. The famous Aldeburgh Music Festival, founded by Britten in 1948, made the barns its new permanent home and shops, holiday accommodation, cafés and tea rooms – and a river tripper boat – have all moved in around the site to create a viable Arts Centre.

We still have an hour of flood in hand by the time we make fast to the wharf at Snape, time for a pint in the Plough & Sail (another one, so closely linked are farming and sail transport in this part of the world). This old sailorman's pub has been saved as a viable concern by the

'Swan' at Snape 1969

new visitor traffic and, although recently extended to cope with increasing numbers, it still has a reasonably atmospheric bar in the old part of the building. Needless to say, pints of Adnams are ordered.

But we cannot linger. Given the tricky navigation and our groundings on our way up, we don't want to get stranded in the middle of nowhere on the way down and decide to leave while there is still a half-hour or so of flood to come. We do just have time, though, for a

'Emily Ann' at Snape 2011

photo call to record the scene as I remembered it when we brought 'Swan' alongside back in 1969. Serendipity now plays its hand in the visit as the half barge 'Cygnet' is moored in that self same spot.

Another foot of water over the mud banks and, as there is no wind down as far as Iken Cliff, our newly learnt previous experience gives us a trouble-free run under engine. There the sun breaks through, the tide has now turned and we make sail once more, close-hauled to the wind, such as it was and mostly tide created.

Then a sea breeze fills in. By sheer chance, another gaff-rigged yacht is up at Barber's Reach and, true to our past sailing careers, the inevitable race is on as with gathering momentum the ebb carries us past the withies swaying gently in the current.

As we approach our mooring again, the last of the yacht club's junior race week fleet are beating back, too, with varying degrees of expertise but plenty of whoops to indicate the fun they are having. Harbour stow is rapidly completed and a VHF call soon brings the club boatman out to us.

Next stop, the friendly yacht club for a cup of tea and a piece of home-made cake. What a fine scene! Kids everywhere and a great view from the clubhouse.

The adults' evening race begins now and several very racy-looking Swallow keelboats – to our eyes more part of the Solent scene than the East Coast – cross the start line while weaving in and out of moored boats. How we wish we could join in this particular piece of typical East Coast magic.

The town of Aldeburgh is well worth a visit with its old moot hall, interesting antique and book shops and a perfectly adequate pub or two. There is also the opportunity of bracing walks along the coastal sea wall, high up above the town, and with the shingle beach to seaward it's almost like being in Holland.

Just a four-minute walk from the yacht club you come to the White Hart. A very striking building, seemingly of oak-beam construction, it also looks as though it should have been at least a Tythe barn. But in fact it's fairly modern, its only nod to history being that the original pub was in the cottage attached to one side. It's a very pubby pub, with no food (except nuts and crisps) and seemingly unaffected by a need to try to cater for the tourist trade. Hence, an interesting range of beers, Adnams, Everards and George Gale, scrubbed wooden tables, old fashioned banquettes, a clientele of local boating characters and interesting sailing, historical and lifeboat pictures on the wall.

Altogether a very pleasant place to round off yet another magical day to Snape and back. Definitely on our 'return to' list.

Robin (left) and Paul yarn up the Alde to Snape

CHAPTER 4

'Time warp town' – or is it?

Southwold recce, the disappearance of Dunwich, the Battle of Sole Bay and Adnams rules, OK!

As far as we know from his 'Magic' book, MG did not sail to Southwold or, if he did, he obviously didn't find it interesting enough to include. We never made it by sea, either, but we considered it as a real option for the harbour of departure for a crossing to the Netherlands. It is the nearest UK point to that country.

We did a full land-based recce but, in the event, the vagaries of the summer weather frustrated the plan and the passage was made from Ipswich instead.

Southwold is not strictly part of the Swatchways proper but it is a charming place and a safe harbour, even if a little tricky to get into. The recce was worth filing for another occasion when the north-easterly winds may be less habitual.

As you approach Southwold by road, as we do, following the north bank of the river Blythe, it feels like entering a strange and separate land. Flat fields on either side seem to form a natural divide to be crossed from the 'mainland'. Dunwich, on the opposite south bank, was once a major port but the sea has swallowed the town up by progressive erosion since 1328 when a storm rendered it useless as a port. It was all gone by 1920 except for a tiny village on the shore, mainly comprising holiday cottages. The Ship Inn notably remains in working order, now more a restaurant/hotel than a pub, but provides a pleasant experience for the land-based visitor.

Southwold has had to withstand its own privations over the centuries, what with a plague and a fire in 1659 which swept away most of the town. It, too, was once an important port for trade and war ships and, classified by the enemy as a fortified town, it was bombarded during the First World War and evacuated during the second.

It is now such a haven of peace and tranquillity, oozing calm and old-world appeal, entering it is like arriving in a time warp. Yet it has a thriving brewery, a harbour busy with boatyards and a working fishing fleet whose catch is available for sale in the black-finished fish shacks along the harbourside road.

Southwold is both surrounding and surrounded by the Adnams family brewery. The craft and concern for the town that wafts from the people in the brew house is absorbed and returned by the rest of the residents.

Visitor pontoons at Southwold

The harbour is a mile away, across more flood flats. It is actually artificial in that, in order to save at least one operational harbour, it was formed by the re-routed River Blyth, diverted when Dunwich disappeared and Southwold's Sole Bay coastline was also steadily eroding.

Sole Bay is famous for the Battle of Sole Bay in 1672 between an English/French joint fleet and the Dutch. The English were caught napping with many sailors ashore in the pubs when the 138 Dutch ships came into view through a thick sea mist. But eventually they got under way, mustering 156 ships, about a third of them French. It must have been a stunning sight for anyone watching from the cliff top.

It was, we are told, a bloody battle with great loss of life on both sides and reports record that corpses were still being washed ashore months later. In the end the home fleet prevailed.

The Martlesham red lion

Many ships had been set on fire or sunk and some were captured. One of these was the 'Stavoren', captured by our ship 'Cambridge'. The 'Stavoren's' figurehead, a bright red lion's head effigy, ended up adorning the Red Lion Inn at Martlesham, a few miles away near Woodbridge and on its own navigable creek off the Deben river. The Red Lion was an important coaching and post inn in those days on the main London to Norwich road. The figurehead is still there to this day and the inn still a popular venue, serving real ales and seasonable menus. Some parts of the building date back to the 16th century, most are 19th century additions, but it's still an attractive, historic building.

In Southwold, the Sole Bay Inn on the cliff above the bay is a place to reflect on the battle. A 'real' pub, full of character, it's on the green opposite the brewery and overlooks the bay. Adnams Ales are, of course, the only 'real' beers served there.

Going down on the river side and into the port takes you on another step back in time, with huts selling fresh fish, small boatyards still offering craft skills, a sailing club, reserved and visitor moorings, the lifeboat station and a rather superior harbour master's office, elevated on stilts. In this office, conversation is constantly interrupted by the VHF as commercial fishing boats and private yachts call in to confirm safe entry or departure from the harbour.

On our visit, a sunny day in early spring, the harbour master is busy painting the outside of his hut, juggling his paint brush and pot with answering the hand-held VHF and calls on his mobile. We manage to get him inside to discuss information for our planned arrival by boat later in the season. "No problems! Just come. We love visitors and we will find you a berth. But there is a bar to be overcome and don't try to get in if an easterly gale's blowing. Also, it's tidal and the tide goes out a fair way. The river remains navigable but gets a bit narrow. So best to arrive with the tide a couple of hours before high water."

His attention is taken again by a yacht on the VHF

asking for permission and advice to come in with about two or three hours of flood still to come. There is instant response from the amenable harbour master: "No problem. There is a fishing boat also coming in so I suggest you let them go first, then follow in behind."

We watch the yacht's progress. A little popple over the bar and she is in, marshes to port, the quay and huts to starboard. As she approaches the moorings, the harbour master is on the VHF again with instruction for berth reference and soon, there she is, safe and snug in her allotted spot.

The pub on the quay, the Harbour Inn, is right opposite the visitor berths. A sociable place, Adnams Ales to the fore, a nice new extension for a dining-room and a children-friendly garden.

An important reminder of the coastal vulnerability is the mark on the wall outside where the flood water of the 1953 East Coast floods rose to, two metres above the ground. Behind the pub, the fields which separate the harbour from the town were completely flooded to more or less the same depth.

The horror of the encroachment of the sea must have been awesome in 1953. Not that Southwold is unused to this. The Battle of Sole Bay with the Dutch was won but the battle with the sea is gradually being lost. Nevertheless, the cliffs now boast an imposing lighthouse, a set of historic canon, some picturesque houses and the delightful beach huts for which the town is

1953 flood line on the Harbour Inn

Gun Hill

famous – selling around the £40k mark!

Up the High Street you come to a pretty square with market stalls and the wonderful Swan Hotel. Walk into the Swan and you go back once again to a former age of elegance. Afternoon tea is taken in the sitting-room. The dining-room has crisp white tablecloths and heavy silver. And in the typical hotel bar, serving the full range of Adnams products, a regular in sports jacket and military-style moustache perches on a stool which is clearly

The Swan Hotel

'his' space. The whole scene sums up the gentility of this town to a tee.

Turn right out of the Swan and right again to find the booking office for brewery tours. The brewery is *the* industry of the town and testament to its commitment to the local population. Adnams owns many of the pubs and hotels as well as producing the beer and maintaining the viability of the town – against the odds, some might say.

A family concern in Southwold since 1857, Adnams could have moved out when they built a new eco-friendly distribution warehouse a couple of miles inland. But they didn't. They committed themselves to their site in the heart of the town – and consequently slightly awkward for modern-size trucks – so as to invest in, support and sustain the commercial viability of Southwold. This commitment was recognised by the award of the OBE to chairman Jonathan Adnams in the 2009 New Year Honours list, which he accepted "on behalf of the whole company".

Industry it may be, but its buildings grouped around

View of the town from the Copper House Distillery

Jonathan Adnams and his stills

the small green are delightfully photogenic, architecturally pleasing and topped by a new glass-panelled tower through which the gleaming new copper stills of the Copper House Distillery can be seen. Adnams is the only brewery in England to have a brewing licence and a spirits distilling licence for the same premises. The real ale is real, the gin is first rate, the barley (not potato) vodka is boutique-like, flavoursome and slightly perfumed, and the whisky is made by a master distiller refugee from the Scotch whisky industry. Still maturing when we are there, it should be interesting. Available from 2013, we are told. Adnams has a terrific retail shop as well, selling all its products, fine wine as well plus smart kitchen paraphernalia.

Back to the harbour for a final check, we find the Royal National Lifeboat Institution station. Over a period of 20 years, Jonathan Adnams served the lifeboat cause, too, as crew and then helmsman. In 1981 and again in 1990 he received RNLI citation awards for his skill in sea rescues of fishing vessels and yachts.

English whisky maturing

Fish sheds on the harbourside road

Along the quay we sample the delightful fish shacks, selling seafood and some of them tea and scones besides. The fish is caught by the local fleet and the shacks are named after each particular boat. Eat there or take away to cook at home or back on-board.

All this awaits the visitor by road or sea. We promise ourselves that next time we will arrive by sea.

CHAPTER 5

'Swan'

An enduring barge yacht

'Swan' circa 1970, Charles at the helm
(photo John Moyes)

There is something about your first real boat, a boat with a cabin, lockers, a galley and somewhere that you can lie down flat. 'Swan' was just that boat to us.

Newly married, I wanted to share the enchantment of the East Coast with my wife and here, I felt, was the perfect boat to do so. 'A barge yacht' said the advertisement on the broker's board.

"Where are her leeboards and sprit?" I asked.

"Ah, internal leeboards, see! She's all double-skinned m'ogany, gaff rigged, see, an' built for racing up th'Thames."

I suppose owning a yacht was stretching our budget but camping under a boom tent in my sailing dinghy had lost its charm. I remember well the day we took over ownership and eased 'Swan' out of the boatyard at Maldon.

The magic worked and we spent our first years together revisiting many of my favourite haunts. I recall the day a salty-looking fellow rowed over, leaned on his oars and asked if this was the same 'Swan' that Griffiths wrote about. I was proud to be able to assure him it was.

The East Coast rivers and creeks that I thought I knew so well continued to delight us. In 'Swan' we were able to sneak up previously unexplored inlets with our plates and rudder half raised. We could anchor in the shallows. With her leeboards hidden within the topsides, we were once mistaken for a little two-and-a-half tonner. An unfortunate keelboat had spotted our riding light and tucked in behind us, unnoticed. In the morning, they were still aground and at a somewhat uncomfortable angle.

She was kind to us, never gave us a scare and in our time we cruised to the Wash, up the Thames to London and even into the inland waterways.

The opportunity to move to New Zealand curtailed our weekend adventures. 'Swan' found herself new owners and she became a fond memory to us.

Wind the clock forward to the new century. When this book was still in the planning stages, I was home in New Zealand when I received an email with the subject heading "SWAN" and a message asking if I was the Charles Scoones who once owned "Swan'. "The same," I replied. "Why?"

For a day or two I imagined all manner of stories.

'Swan' – a sorry sight at Leigh

'Swan' would now have to be at least a century old, if indeed she was still afloat.

The writer Jon was researching her past. It seems that his grandfather had been an owner and she had passed into family folklore. Had I any pictures, he asked, where and when, etc, etc. I learned that 'Swan' was lying forgotten at the back of a boatyard at Leigh-on-Sea, Essex. His plan was to restore her.

A few months later I was in England. We met and I went to take a look. A blue tarpaulin covered our poor 'Swan'. She had rotten holes in her deck and there was little paint left on her hull. The bronze tackle blocks that once hauled up the steel leeboards had been pilfered and the little oval brass builder's plate was missing from the cockpit coaming. I remember the thrill of polishing it and revealing the well worn words "Alfred Burgoine Chiswick 1897". The cabin had been stripped and dank rainwater lay in the bilge. In my time I have been involved in a few boat projects but this one to me looked like a lost cause!

I offered some hollow words of encouragement and

Lantern slide of 'Swan' circa 1908

handed Jon some of my pictures showing 'Swan' under sail and my favourite image, in holiday mode, moored alongside at the Snape Maltings.

I walked away, savouring my memories.

Then, in 2009, home once more in New Zealand, I received another excited email from Jon with pictures attached of her being craned out of the yard and on her way to Lowestoft on the back of a truck. She had been accepted by the International Boatbuilding Training College there as a worthy restoration project. She was regarded as 'a rare example of Victorian boatbuilding'.

On our next visit to England I had another excuse to head off to the northern borders of Suffolk. In my mind, I expected to see a small yard with perhaps two or three projects underway. That is the way I remember the boatyards of Burnham. But here on the banks of Oulton Broad was a bounty of classic yachts and launches, all being lovingly restored or waiting in the wings, in a glorious maze of boatsheds. Students bent over benches in the jointing shop were learning the traditional skills before being allowed to even touch a real boat.

Ready for restoration at Lowestoft with new owner Jon

'Swan's' current owner Jon had enrolled as an apprentice himself. Proudly he took me to see her, now safely under cover and waiting her turn to be reborn. Over a boatyard cup of tea, I learned that the story had yet another connection, a quirky twist.

It seemed that after I had sold 'Swan' and moved overseas, she sailed out of Benfleet for a few seasons before sadly becoming neglected. Then a young chap Toby spotted her and, ignoring warnings from his dad not to buy a boat with crabs running around in the bilges, gave her another lease on life, renewing much of her rotting keel. Eventually he, too, moved on to bigger boats.

Unknowingly at the time, it was the same Toby who had recently helped us haul out 'Antiope' in Fambridge. A chance comment over a cuppa filled in another bit of history. One day, I thought, perhaps I might even get an invitation to take the tiller of our beloved 'Swan' once more.

CHAPTER 6

Harwich for the Continent...

Maritime heritage, the Ship, the Butt & Oyster and a passage to Vlissingen

'Long red every six, the Deane buoy,' confirms my crew as we head out to sea from Harwich harbour late in the day. Passing by the dark silhouette of the buoy, I note the time on the chart.

Months of refitting now behind us, we are at last on our way to 'the other side'. As we head east, the sea is like a mirror reflecting the setting sun behind us.

The Deane buoy is one of the channel marks guiding shipping into Harwich harbour and Felixstowe Docks. My mother was a Deane, her Harwich forebears including Sir Anthony Deane who was joint MP with Samuel Pepys at the time when Pepys was secretary to the Navy. The Deanes were master shipwrights and for generations made a living plying the North Sea to Holland. It seems fitting that we are making our own departure from Harwich.

Turbulent weather has plagued the North Sea for the past month and a lull between fronts looks like our best window for the crossing for several weeks to come. We do have the benefit of a weather forecast, diesel engines and GPS, things that Maurice Griffiths managed without when he made the same crossing in 'Juanita', described by him as 'a little Falmouth yawl'.

His crossing took 35 hours and entailed struggling through calms, fog and foul tides before eventually anchoring in Ostend harbour. No floating pontoons then as there are now. Our passage is to take less than half the time to Flushing, but not without its own dramas.

Our craft 'Antiope' is a shallow draft, 14 metre steel motorboat, ideal for the inland waters of Europe but not really designed for offshore. So prudence and strong lobbying from the crew dictate when conditions are okay to go.

It is while waiting for the right weather to make our crossing that we have some time to explore the area we are leaving. I have to admit that, when sailing up to Suffolk in my youth, the focus was usually getting to Pin Mill and the Butt & Oyster before closing time. Back then, history and the local family connections were not high on my list of interests. Cruising the River Orwell today, I find that it still has the same old charm. Yes, there are now marinas but they do not intrude. Ipswich Haven Marina becomes our home for a few days, a remarkable

Waiting for the weather in Levington marina

The Ship Inn

transformation from the desolate docks I remember.

The town serves us well for provisioning for our big adventure. However, for a change of scenery and to be closer to the sea and our passage, we pop down to Suffolk Yacht Harbour at Levington. It is a very windy period and the Classic Yachts are trying to have a regatta. They do, with lots of reefs in their sails, but it is too windy for our boat to make the passage across the North Sea. We stay tied up and the Haven Ports Yacht Club lightship clubhouse makes us very welcome.

We also walk up the hill to revisit the Ship Inn. It is on entering this little pub again that I have one of those déjà vu moments.

Back in my dinghy sailing days, we had been told by the locals in the Butt & Oyster to take the tide up Levington creek to the old barge wharf and walk up the lane to the Ship. The creek is still there but largely subsumed by the marina. The creek was, and still is really, only suitable for a 15ft centreboard dinghy or these days perhaps a sea kayak, now popular for exploring estuaries and tidal coastal rivers.

The tiny bar that it was then was like a cosy farmhouse kitchen and beer was dispensed through a hatch. Today, the Ship survives as a popular restaurant and its patrons in the know arrive by car down the narrow lanes. I duck under the low beam into the old bar room, now a little snug with the same old iron fireplace, and for a moment I am back in the 60s with a pint for two bob.

We take the opportunity to explore Harwich. A new pontoon at the old Halfpenny Pier now welcomes visitors to town, in contrast to the time when getting ashore was a contest with the tugs, commercial ferries and local fishermen. It was easier then to press on up the Orwell to Pin Mill.

Across the road, the Pier Hotel is resplendent once more. Travellers through the years waited here for the time to board their packet boat and the maritime heritage of this busy port is evident all around. The 'Mayflower' first sailed from Harwich for the New World. Much later, Frobisher set sail from here to chart the North West passage.

Trinity House quay and pier

Since 1812 Trinity House has had a depot here, servicing the lights and buoys along the coast, and Harwich is now the Trinity House Operational Headquarters. Henry VIII granted the Corporation a charter in 1514 and light dues are still charged to shipping. I remember when half a

The old high lighthouse

Plaque at the end of 'the Essex Way'

dozen off duty lightships swung at anchor up the Stour. Now there is just one, plus a couple apparently undergoing refits alongside the Trinity House pier. It is, however, a delight still to find many of them around the coast, providing homes for yacht clubs, like the one we enjoyed in Levington Marina, and also for scout troops and sailing schools.

A walk around the old town does not take long. Pepys, a frequent visitor, stayed here. Nelson slept there. A pub on every corner, although many are now private houses. Down one narrow street, I find a tall redbrick tower, the high lighthouse built in 1818 as one of the leading lights to the harbour. Redundant now due to the shifting sands, a plaque fixed to the brickwork proclaims this is the end of 'the Essex Way', an 81-mile walking route from Epping. Quite a trek by my standards!

The old lifeboat station nearby also became redundant and now serves as the lifeboat museum, housing a former Clacton lifeboat and other historical artifacts.

The current RNLI lifeboat station is now on the harbour side, opposite the Pier Hotel, with its own free visitor centre to view the new boats and pictures of heroic rescues made in the past.

The Navy yard once built ships here for Nelson's fleet. Nelson was no stranger to Harwich. He once found himself weatherbound here, under orders to sail to Sheerness in Kent but unable to weather the Cork Sands in the persistent easterlies. He sought local knowledge from a surveyor, Graham Spence, and, putting to sea in the frigate 'Medusa', managed to find a passage sailing close-hauled through a shallow channel, close under the Naze headland at Walton. Thus the 'Medusa Channel' gained its name. It now has navigation buoys so that we can all find it, just as we did when we sailed from Maldon to the Walton Backwaters, passing the Medusa buoy and through the channel as we made up to the Pye End buoy.

I remember the Eastern Region British Rail poster 'Harwich for the Continent', the romantic view of the night packet waiting alongside at Parkeston Quay for the boat train from London.

As a lad I watched the ferries sweep by from the deck of my father's yacht as we entered the harbour after a long day's sail from the Crouch. They were on their way to The Hook, Zeebrugge, or even Denmark. It was probably my first serious voyage and a great adventure when I, too, eventually set sail for the 'other side' with dad aboard 'Bonita', down the Orwell and out to sea past the busy docks. Arthur Ransome's book 'We Didn't Mean to go to Sea' had set the scene for me.

In later years, Harwich became a familiar starting point as I found myself crewing on various go-fast racing yachts, the navigation left to others, as we thrashed our way to Rotterdam or Ostend.

Back to the present and our hopes are for a calm passage. So far so good and we make excellent progress as the night closes in around us. The wind farms clearly mark the sand banks, adding another dimension to navigation. By midnight we have reached the traffic-separation zones and dutifully cross at right angles, which shifts the residual swell from the recent storms on to our beam. The crew become quiet, wedging themselves into corners as 'Antiope' takes on a steady roll and the galley rattles for a while until pots and jars find new homes.

Once clear of the lanes, we have just relaxed and resumed a more comfortable course when what appears to be the lights of a ferry boat show up on our starboard quarter. "Where is she off to outside the shipping lanes?" says I. "Better give her some room," I thinks, as her lights grow in scale. Soon it becomes clear that this is no mere channel ferry. In the first glow of dawn we can finally make out her red and black funnel.

The 'Queen Elizabeth' cruise ship passes ahead of 'Antiope'

Cunard's 'Queen Elizabeth' cruise liner comes abeam, passes ahead and then turns gracefully across our bow.

Another forest of windmills ahead signals our approach to the Netherlands. Finally, 12 hours after passing the Deane buoy, tired but incredibly pleased to have made it, we enter the lock at Vlissingen.

We were grateful for our engines, chart-plotter and the comfort of an enclosed wheelhouse, our passage made without the challenges that Maurice had faced during his crossing. And remembering his trip to nearby Ostend had taken him 35 hours, I didn't feel too guilty. I've done my time out there perched on the weather rail or hunched over a wheel, ducking each blast of cold spray the North Sea had to throw at us.

The Swatchways for now are behind us as we set out to work the Dutch inland waterways and canals, but I know we will be back to them soon. The Dutch waterways are interesting, historic, architecturally attractive, friendly and different but, we think, not really magical like our Swatchways back in Britain.

CHAPTER 7

Secret waters to share

Deep into the Walton Backwaters with the Warden

We had already visited Walton Backwaters – Hamford Water on the chart – with 'Antiope' en route to our Ipswich destination but were constrained by draft and tide and a degree of nervousness on our first visit in a big boat here. We only explored halfway up Walton Channel before turning around to anchor, after a gentle and not too long-lived grounding in the mud, in Kirby Creek off Hamford Water and next day headed off to Ipswich.

Today's visit to the Backwaters was planned around high tide and with an expert pilot for a detailed exploration of every creek and island and areas normally inaccessible to visitors, to parts that even MG never reached – nevertheless, just the sort of anchorage he would have loved.

To do this we are introduced by Bill Gibbon, local Walton & Frinton Yacht Club member and a Trustee of the Yacht Trust, which owns the land area it occupies, to Leon Woodrow. As Warden of the Backwaters, Leon has agreed to let us in on the secrets of conservation and navigable water, at least at high tide. These are the locations for Arthur Ransome's 'Secret Water'. His eighth book in the Swallows and Amazons series, it was first published in 1939, a few years after MG's 'Magic of the

Swatchways'. We might conjecture that Ransome, a sailor himself, had been influenced by MG's stories.

Chris Opperman, a volunteer assistant warden and keen conservationist and bird 'twitcher', comes along, too, and he can easily correlate the islands and 'red sea' featured in the 'Secret Water' to the actual islands and creeks as we cruise them. This is a wonderful safe water playground, tidal but flat water, deep enough in parts even at low water for a keel yacht up to 50ft, but more ideally suited to shallow-draft yachts, centreboard dinghies or cruising kayaks. A paradise for bird and wildlife watchers.

The cranes of Felixstowe port are visible across the marshes from more or less anywhere on the Backwaters. We called them 'giraffes on the horizon' when we came here before. Chris sees them every day and calls them his 'dinosaurs'. "It's amazing," he declares, "that the biggest container port in the country is only a mile or two away and yet here it is always so quiet and peaceful and feels quite remote." No reply to that other than silently to wonder at it.

Our vessel for this trip is the Warden's launch which we find alongside at Titchmarsh Marina. Dug out of the marshes, the marina is now of some size and busy, with most berths taken and many boats still ashore, hoisted there by hydraulic Renner lift. Yet it nestles into the surrounding green-topped mud banks, hardly disturbing the scenery, certainly not the flock of swallows that seems to be dive-bombing our heads as we wait to board. Yes, the swallows are here. We can be the Amazons!

Titchmarsh delivers the best that marinas do, clubhouse café/bar, chandlery, laundry and a range of marine services. If you want to arrive by road with a trailed boat to explore the Backwaters, thus avoiding the passage from the open sea, from the efficiency perspective this is the place to come to.

What, we wondered later in the day, over a pint in the Walton & Frinton Yacht Club, would MG's view of marinas have been? "Ah," said Chris, who works in radio and used to be involved with a sailing publication, "I was lucky enough to interview him back in the 70s and asked him that very question. I expected him to be disparaging but he said without hesitation he was all for them.

"He thought they did an excellent job of supporting, even fuelling an expansion in the boating industry through cruising yachts and performed a great and necessary part of that. As editor of 'Yachting Monthly' he naturally supported anything that helped the UK boating industry. But he couldn't totally change his spots. He went on to say part of the reason he liked them was that it kept all these new boats away from his favourite creeks so that they remained quiet and lovely."

Walton Backwaters is a protected area, bird sanctuary and wild life reserve. Being Warden is a full-time job to "keep an eye" on the area, according to Leon, keep boat speeds under check to reduce erosion of the soft mud banks and generally help visitors and locals enjoy but not damage this beautiful, fragile area. The Warden is appointed by Tendring Council but the cost is subsidised by contributions from local businesses, bird and nature conservation societies and local benefactors. The Warden has powers to prosecute but no-one has been in the 20 years Leon has been in the job. "Long may it last that way," he says. He does it all with advice

On Stone Point

and persuasion and his methods work well.

We set off from Titchmarsh Marina just two hours before high water, down the Twizzle into Walton Channel to land on the beach at Stone Point, our first stop. This is a privately owned promontory but visiting by dinghy is allowed, even walking dogs ashore, as long as you keep to the tracks and take away droppings. With grassy marsh on top, the point itself is a fine stretch of shingly beach, very steep to. The channel marker buoy is only a stone's throw off the edge and in a deep draft boat you have to hold your nerve to pass very close to the shore. But the water is definitely there. And anyone lazing on the beach has a steady stream of boats to watch as they make their way past in one direction or the other.

Opposite is Horsey Island, edged here by a row of 18 sunken lighters filled with shingle and holed to sink them to try to slow down the erosion of the mud banks. When you arrive, entering the Hamford Water channel from Pye End buoy, they look mysterious and foreboding, derelict and unintentional. Since they were sunk there 20 years ago, they have helped but erosion continues, as does the consequent silting up of the waters. Now cash-strapped local authorities are withdrawing finances to maintain and repair the banks, opting to let nature take its course.

This seems to forecast a time when there will be too little navigable water for larger boats. The encroachment of land will eventually triumph over sea. Ironically, it is the total opposite of the sea triumphing over land and swallowing up most of Dunwich, Suffolk's 'lost town', further north up the coast by Southwold. Years away, maybe, but the message is clear…Go and visit the Backwaters now!

Our shore stay on Stone Point over, we reboard the launch, push off and head north again along Walton Channel to turn to port at Island Point north cardinal buoy and into Hamford Water. This buoy is the apex of the exit/entry channel from Pye End buoy. On our last visit, we came right around Pye End just to make sure we found the deep water river hidden from view under the wide expanse of visible water. But Chris asserts that coming from the south, the Blackwater or the Colne, it is safe to enter leaving the No 2 red to port, saving quite a distance. We make a mental note but add that this is probably only for expert locals, although we can imagine MG using it. Next time I expect we will still close the Pye End buoy.

Navigating out is well buoyed but off Stone Point the red and green buoys seem to be in a straight line. They are, as the channel requires a sharp S-bend chicane wiggle to take it. Exciting on the first go but comfortable enough for our local experts.

Heading westward, the Hamford Water feels quite

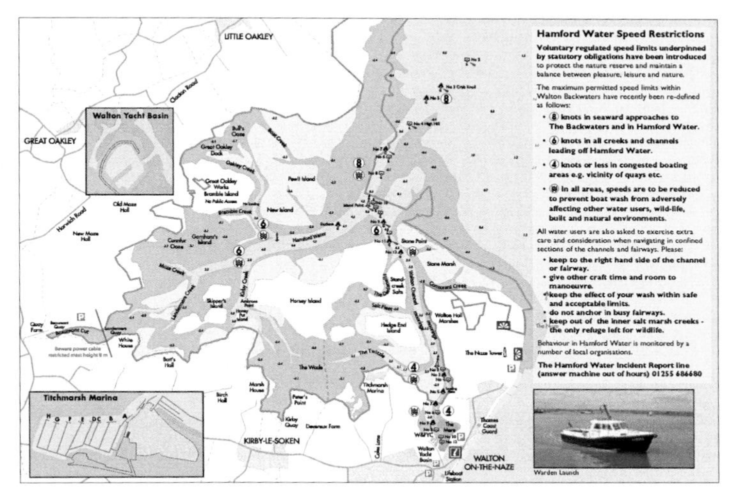

Map from Bill Wilkinson's Walton Backwaters Guide
©Community & Conservation Trust

deep and the charts offer four metres plus at low tide. It is very sheltered and a few sizeable offshore yachts are anchored here. Several lugsail dinghies of 'Swallows and Amazons' type are also enjoying the sunny day, pleasant breeze and flat water. They look picturesque and quaint, almost a film set of the past, and the young sailors are obviously having fun. They wave gaily to us as we pass by and wave back, assuming this is a friendly gesture and not a warning of pirates ahead!

The Pye End buoy is maintained by the harbour authorities, as is Island Point north cardinal and Bramble Creek east cardinal, but the hidden sand banks are irregular and to navigate safely and with confidence needs more guidance. This is provided by privately funded and maintained port and starboard buoys from No 2 after Pye End to No 13 beyond Stone Point in Walton Channel and the Exchem buoy in the main

Hamford Water channel. The sponsorship comes from local businesses, the marina and the yacht club. Further on into the Backwaters, some help is provided by stick withies. The rest is up to you, your intuition, your depth sounder and a reliable chart and guide.

We turn northward and to starboard again on the East cardinal buoy to enter Bramble Creek. This buoy is maintained by the harbour authority because a commercial ship comes up on a regular schedule to Bramble Island and the Great Oakley Works, a large plant producing specialist explosives. The whole island, therefore, is strictly off limits. The chemicals used are dangerous and transporting by sea avoids the risks associated with transport by road. Thus, years on, the practice of sailing cargo barges winkling up tiny tidal creeks for commerce is perpetuated, except now the load is carried in small coasters with several times the capacity of the old sailing barges.

Off the landing quay and dominating in the flat surroundings is a high iron turning post so that the ships turn ready to face downstream before being loaded. The warning notices, the empty jetty and the complete absence of humans give the whole place the aura of a James Bond thriller. We pass by, resisting the temptation to pretend we are enemy spies and land illegally – after all, we do have the Warden with us. So we continue on into areas only navigable near high tide, even for our small boat, along what is now Oakley Creek, then into Bull's Ooze and Boat Creek.

There are private jetties and dinghy moorings here, accessed through the farm on the marshes, but no humans today. The 'dinosaur' cranes of Felixstowe can be seen but the creek feels more remote and mysterious than anywhere else in the Backwaters. A small centre-boarder could moor over-tide but taking the mud is inevitable for anything but a short stay.

We turn and retreat back down the creek. There is more we need to explore. We turn west again at the Bramble East cardinal buoy and head up the Hamford Water which becomes Landermere Creek, bypassing Kirby Creek for the moment. Here, lining the banks, is an amazing colony of seals, their fur a bright ginger colour. They are a phenomenon unique to these creeks. Local folklore says their hue is due to their lazing in the mud which has high iron deposits in it. Rusty seals? As all the pups are light grey, this seems hard to verify but nevertheless the adult colourings are spectacular. About a hundred of them. The Warden says the area could sustain many more, maybe up to a thousand.

They lie ungainly on the top of the banks. After all, they've had to climb up five-foot by flipper, not simply slither up as they do on the banks of Foulness Island on the River Crouch. They watch us in our boat, interested, a little wary, ready to slide into the water if we get

Seals enjoy the Backwaters

too close. In the water, so agile and elegant, playful and amusing. Ashore, flopped, lazy, ungainly and apparently sunbathing. They swim out to sea to find fish to feed on and return to the creek to live.

There are two species in the colony: Classic Greys, with heads like horses, and Common Seals with heads like Labrador dogs. But here at least both species are ginger so perhaps the local theory is right – it just takes a season or two for the red to get into the blood and colour up the fur.

There is water to moor up here. A 40ft Hansa is moored near to an 18ft clinker Salcombe Yawl, far from home but the hull typically East Coast-like, similar to the 18ft clinker sailing one-designs of Harwich, Brightlingsea and Southend and the Jewels of Walton & Frinton Yacht Club.

At anchor is an intriguing Dutch sailing ketch whose hull looks more like a 1930s' straight-stemmed gentleman's steam yacht. Steel but with slight vertical rust streaks, she looks in need of a refit, a somewhat dated classic but distinctive at the same time. Many visitors from Holland and Belgium come to the Backwaters, reciprocating our trips to their inland waterways. One or two are from sailing schools with pupils no doubt gaining their Yachtmaster Offshore Competence certificates or something similar.

On her own mooring, signifying she is in her home port, is a cute ketch with an interesting Dutch-barge-style sheer to her lines. This is the 'Stenoa', a sailing yacht now but she was once an RNLI lifeboat and went with the Dunkirk Little Ships fleet of 1940. All these years later, she is smart and well cared for.

At the head of the creek is Landermere Quay. It's

'Stenoa'

little more than a beach but reachable by foot from the mainland. Suitable to keep a rowing dinghy to get to the bigger boats moored in the deeper waters or for Mirror dinghies and suchlike for the kids, as our facilitator Bill had done when his were young.

Further up you come to Beaumont Quay, a cut dug in 1832 to get the barges as near to the road as possible. It was constructed, they say, with stones from the old, demolished London Bridge, brought here as ballast in sailing barges and left behind when they loaded up with grain and lime for the return trip to London. This substantial quay, however, is already victim to the silting process and no longer accessible.

Landermere Quay still functions, though. The large building there was once the King's Head pub – gone now but you can picnic on the beach below it. To the east, nestling among the trees, is a pink house, home of a direct descendent of the great Charles Darwin who had many connections to our Swatchways. His ship 'The Beagle' ended her days in Paglesham, first as a 'watch boat', providing accommodation for Revenue men, but

now sadly swallowed up by the creekside mud.

We head north-east downstream again and halfway turn to starboard into Kirby Creek. At high tides a Mirror dinghy could sail through to the Twizzle, home to Titchmarsh Marina. As for us, shallow draft we may be, but we go aground a little short of The Wade. This low-tide causeway can bear vehicles leading off a lane from Kirby-le-Soken across the creek to Horsey Island, the very same that we were looking at from our Stone Point landing. The locals call it 'Horzy'. Why they don't say 'Horse-y', just the way it is, is anybody's guess! It is conjectured to be the island featured in 'Secret Water' as the campsite. Not so secret now, Horsey hosts a private air strip. But there is no air traffic today and apparently it is hardly used, certainly not enough to scare away the birdlife.

At the head of the creek are the remains of a quay, now called Kirby Hard and only accessible by dinghy for a couple of hours either side of the tide. It connects to a public footpath leading to The Street in Kirby-le-Soken village at a point conveniently midway between two pubs. Yes, two to choose from but only time for a swift libation if you're going to beat the tide!

Kirby Creek offers reasonable depth, two metres at its entrance but as deep as 3.8 further up by Honey Pot Island. When we visited in 'Antiope', we accepted safe depth near the entrance, too cautious to probe further. But now we know where to go next time. This is solitude in the extreme and a delightful, magical place to anchor up.

We retrace our route, past Honey Pot Island with Skipper's Island to port, owned and controlled by Essex Wildlife Trust, and back to the Island Point North cardinal to turn through 90 degrees to the south, back into Walton Channel. Compared with where we have just been, this is busy!

The channel is well buoyed, thanks to Walton & Frinton Yacht Club, and there is a double line of moorings all the way. The passageway of deep water between is clear but a bit squeezed. The boats are varied and interesting, mostly sail, mostly about 28 to 35ft, with a 38ft maximum imposed by the yacht club and the Warden.

If you anchor or moor in this part of Walton Channel, the easiest landing point is Eagles Hard. It's privately owned but the public can use it. It gives access to the town and a pleasant circular walk round the sea wall, taking in the Naze Tower.

Keep going up. The Twizzle bears round to the west but continue straight on and the Walton Channel, narrower now as a creek, leads to the splendid Walton & Frinton Yacht Club. Leave the north cardinal buoy at the Twizzle junction close to starboard – do not cut across as it marks a very long underwater shallow spit. Titchmarsh Marina up the Twizzle can be accessed at all

Walton & Frinton Yacht Club – soon to be rebuilt

states of the tide but practical access to the yacht club quay is limited to a couple of hours either side of high tide.

The club welcomes visitors. The quay outside happily accommodates a small yacht such as a Stella but staying is restricted to two hours for crew 'refreshing and refreshment', as the club regulations put it. Boats then have to move off to deeper water or to the 'Pond', the yacht basin further upstream. Or, on the other side of this creek, the Halls & Son and Bedwell boatyards (separate operations) have quays where boats can request to lie alongside and dry out. The yards offer yacht services and lifting gear.

On the other side of the yacht club buildings, in the eastern arm of the creek, are floating finger jetties where the 14ft Jewel class one-design fleet is moored. This boat was designed in 1947 by Robbie Stone from Brightlingsea who designed the larger 18ft Brightlingsea One Design as well. Both very much along the same lines, centreboarders, clinker built, three-quarter decked and pretty! The Jewel fell out of favour but is now

Jewels on the dock

being revived. Many old Jewels are being found around the country, bought, renovated and repatriated to the Walton & Frinton fleet. Brightly painted, they make a picture-postcard scene beside the club.

We are there during Cadet Week with youngsters in Mirrors, Lasers, Topazes and the like racing around the narrow confines between the moorings and generally enjoying themselves. Prize-giving takes place once the tide has gone.

A few metres further on reveals the best bit for the cruising yachtsman. The tidal gated dock known as 'the Pond' contains a constant two metres of water and floating pontoons to moor to fore and aft. Lock in to here (by arrangement with Bedwell & Co which manages it for Walton & Frinton Yacht Trust) and you are staying within a short stroll of the town of Walton-on-the-Naze. "Nearest place to a curry," they say, plus seaside beaches, the pier and pubs.

Not that you need town pubs as the yacht club delivers a fine selection of local 'guest' ales and popular lagers and provides a very respectable bar menu. It

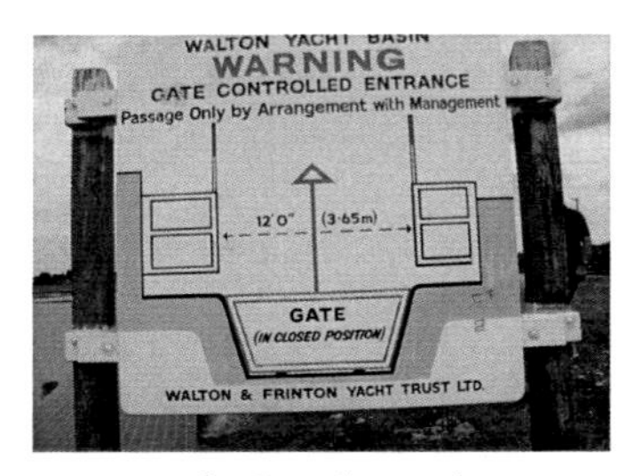

Entry to the Pond moorings

must be one of the friendliest clubs around. The fees are very reasonable. You can come for a few days or join the club and lay up for the winter.

We settle into the bay window overlooking the dinghy dock to talk about the Swatchways and MG. An old friend sails past the window on his way to a deeper mooring. It's 'Andromeda' owned by Richard Woodman, a renowned author of meticulously accurate Naval battle stories and maritime novels and a huge enthusiast of our Swatchway waters. That definitely puts the A1 seal of quality on the place.

The club has launching ramps but adjacent is the Town Hard where you can launch or retrieve trailed boats. Bring a modest lifting keel cruiser here and you could spend a week of tides exploring the Backwaters without ever experiencing waves more than a few inches high – and see something different every day.

Originally, the yacht club quay was for barges moving corn and flour from the windmill which stood on this site. The whole peninsula, Pond and surrounding fields down the creek are owned by the Yacht Trust, set up to ensure they are retained for the purposes of an active yacht club. The club rents the site from the Trust and thus these aims are met. The clubhouse has been extended over the years and is interestingly quirky, but plans to rebuild are in the pipeline.

This is a fabulous destination for summer or winter cruising. One end quite busy with bars and food and laundry (in the marina) and the other end isolated and peaceful. It is tightly controlled but the Warden is friendly and there to help visiting and resident boats and protect the wildlife. It is tidal and the mud may get you. It can be dangerous and the advice is never to try to walk ashore if you are stranded. Just put out an anchor and settle down to enjoy the sights and sounds of the Backwaters until the next tide releases you. Count it as enforced relaxation!

The navigation is well marked if you follow the buoys and withies, although a tad tricky. But this book is not a pilot book – it is a story book to whet your appetite to go. Best get local advice and get a copy of the 'Walton Backwaters – The Users Guide to Secret Water' available from Titchmarsh Marina, the yacht club and local tourist offices. It is informative, interesting and illustrated with photos of the area and invaluable clear charts.

The yacht club provides its own detailed directions to the club quay and the Pond or contact Bedwell's which manages moorings and movements there.

Not so secret now! Get there soon!

Peaceful Kirby Creek

CHAPTER 8

The allure of the River Colne

First stop Brightlingsea, St Osyth and the Pyefleet

Unlike some of our other trips of discovery, this visit is more of a homecoming, bringing back happy memories of childhood summers spent on and around Brightlingsea Creek. So, yes, nostalgia abounds but, like everywhere else, waters and shorelines are constantly changing and new developments, whether natural or man-made, never cease to draw us back there.

We are coming down south-westwards from Harwich. After Clacton, we turn right at the Colne Bar buoy to pick up Colne Point Buoy to starboard, with the Inner Bench Head to port. These are the marks defining the entry to the River Colne.

The Colne has much to attract the cruising sailor. Upon arrival, at Brightlingsea Creek there are moorings, a town with shops and a supermarket, pubs, the Colne Yacht Club and an alongside fuel dock. Alternatively, Pyefleet Creek, opposite at East Mersea Island, offers a magical quiet anchorage surrounded by marshes and the usual stunning East Coast sunsets. Or you can head up river to Wivenhoe to moor on the floating jetty at the very friendly Wivenhoe Sailing Club or, round just one more bend, tie up on the tide alongside the green-grassed quays either side of the Anchor pub at Rowhedge.

With a couple of beaches to moor off as well, where you can go ashore to walk, explore, sunbathe or barbecue, or even scrub the bottom, you have enough for a week of cruising without ever leaving the river.

From the Colne Bar the river runs nearly straight, roughly north-west, for about two miles. Bateman's Tower, prominent on the north side of the Brightlingsea Creek entrance, is a convenient landmark visible all the way up. The next mile or so is a gentle curve before the winding bends of the upper river begin.

Most days, yachts can fetch in or out of the river on the one tack. This is what made the river so convenient for the Thames sailing barges in their trading hey days and Brightlingsea and Pyefleet Creek are favourite destinations for them still on their pleasure cruises and for the annual Colne Barge Match. Just off East Mersea Point or in the lower Pyefleet are always popular weekend anchoring spots. Several smacks make the Pyefleet their regular home mooring and a Thames barge or two seems to be anchored off Bateman's every

A smack reaches into the Colne, the now defunct Bradwell Power Station in the distance

day of the week in the season.

Entering the Colne, Brightlingsea is a logical first port of call if you don't go straight to the Pyefleet. Constant changes in the shifting sands have silted up the entrance to the creek in recent years. The old Creek Mouth Buoy used to float in the middle of the entrance and line up with leading marks on the shore. It's still there but has been joined by an extra post planted on the end of the south-side mud flats off the shingle bank of the entrance, the channel now between them.

The post nearly dries out at spring low tides and yachts not quite getting the entrance right is a daily occurrence, annoying for the crew but great entertainment for onlookers ashore. Best to avoid dead low water going in or out. Once over the entry bar, the rest of the creek has pretty good water. But it is usually very full right up the south branch with boats moored fore and aft to piles which have floating mini jetties in between them.

Visitors to Brightlingsea need to call the Harbour Master on the VHF to get a mooring position. He prides himself on hardly ever having to declare 'house full' and will direct you to a berth on one of the floating pontoons between the first sets of piles, roughly where the fishing boats used to moor 60-plus years ago.

Eventually, this creek leads to St Osyth where the boatyard is home to several Thames barges. There was once a tide water-mill there and Thames barges crept up 'Toosey' Creek, as St Osyth is called in the local dialect, under their own sail power. Now they get there and back with a tug launch and it's still a tight squeeze.

Navigating is restricted to either side of high tide but getting up or down is best done Swallows and

Amazons-style in a dinghy – rowing, sailing or with an outboard motor. It's a true Swatchways explorers' trip, winding between the marshes to eventually reach the boatyard.

The creek is dammed off with a road across and the retained mill pond behind where there is water skiing and a little café/bar. The nearest pubs, two to choose from, are a short walk in the direction of the village. St Osyth is worth a visit to see the Norman flint church of St Peter and St Paul and the fine gatehouse of St Osyth Priory. The priory itself, which dates from the 12th century, needs extensive restoration and is no longer open to the public. Keep an eye on the time as the tide drops quickly and Toosey Creek soon becomes little more than a stream.

The public ferry plies across the creek to and from Brightlingsea to Stone Point on the St Osyth side and operates a timetable over to East Mersea, too. A water taxi serves the mooring pontoons – contacts made by mobile phone or VHF. Otherwise, it's a dinghy launching. On the Brightlingsea side there is space for dinghies on the town jetty or a short way upstream on the Colne Yacht Club floating jetty. Visiting yachtsmen welcome.

On the St Osyth side there is the shingle Stone Point, then marshes running up to the sea wall. In summer, creep along the walkable edge of these marshes and the spit at the right state of tide and you will find bountiful crops of wild green samphire. Salt marsh samphire, not to be confused with 'rock samphire', is delicious fresh from the beach and straight into the boiling pot.

Don't pull up the whole plant. Pick the branches off, rinse in fresh cold water, then two minutes in boiling water and a knob of butter is quite sufficient – a little

Toys for the boys and girls on St Osyth Point Clear beach

longer later on in the season as it toughens up somewhat. Don't add salt – it's already salty enough! Pull the stork through your teeth or run your fingers down it and little bud-like flowers come off like grains of rice. Sometimes known as 'the asparagus of the sea', it's tasty, very healthy and free. In smart London restaurants it costs several pounds a portion.

While on this side, it's worth walking up the track and over the sea wall, with its row of wall-top chalets curving round along the Point Clear beach line. There, next to yet another Ferry Boat Inn, is a fine Martello Tower indicating that Stone Point and Brightlingsea had some defence importance when the big agenda was to prepare against a possible Napoleonic invasion. Thanks to Nelson, that never happened, but the tower was taken into military service 150 or so years later as a World War II observation platform.

Brightlingsea is a 'member' of the Cinque Ports network. A charter granted in 1442 makes it subordinate to Sandwich, with responsibilities to assist with defence of the kingdom and providing ships for service in the king's Navy. The mayor of Brightlingsea is referred to as 'the Deputy', the full title being 'Deputy to the Mayor of Sandwich'.

The Point Clear Martello Tower is now a splendid museum set up by local enthusiasts who act as guides and proudly recall the role the tower and the community played back in the 1940s. It's bursting with history and memorabilia from the past two centuries, mostly found locally and mainly military, with a strong focus on aviation. There is a fine view from the typical flat roof as well so definitely worthy of a visit. Entry is free but contributions for upkeep much appreciated.

Walk on straight up the old concrete road, left over from the wartime occupation of this area as a Naval supply base, and you come to Tony's fresh fish 'garage shop'. Tony goes out fishing locally Monday to Wednesday and sells from the garage Thursday through Sunday. Local produce at its best, reasonably priced, and goes very nicely with the free samphire!

On the other hand, on the way back, a handy fish'n'chips take-away bar is right next to the pub. They

Brightlingsea hard – the classic view, crabbing in process

cook to order so sometimes in the summer there is a queue. Get your order in and then, while it's cooking, you should have time for a quick pint in the Ferry Boat to work up an appetite.

Back on Stone Point, a mobile phone call will get the public ferry boat to come and pick you up to go back over to Brightlingsea. A mini, motorised, drop-down, front-end, landing craft, for £1 per passenger (at the time of writing) it crosses to the hammerhead on the floating jetty at all states of the tide.

The jetty itself is very popular for crabbing. Children and often adults, too, crowd along it with their legs dangling over the edge, changing sides as the tide turns. "No crabbing this side," says the sign on the ebb tide side at the top of the jetty. But the tide has its own routine superior to any human intervention and the crabbers follow nature regardless.

Years ago, in Brightlingsea, the ferry service used to be a small fleet of half a dozen 14-16ft clinker built rowing boats, operated by licensed ferrymen, all old sailormen of some sort. Sometimes we were allowed to take the oars ourselves – the early learning of seamanship skills in action.

The row boats had their name on a board in the stern. 'J Wood, licensed to carry 6' was one. He only had one leg, rumoured to be a war injury, and an arm crutch like Long John Silver, so of course was known as 'Old Peg Leg'. He was a bit grumpy but I marvelled at the athletic way he had to swing himself off the jetty and into his boat. The fare was tuppence (2d or two old pence) each way in those days.

Another was 'A Bowles – licensed for 7'. Captain Arthur was my main mentor and occasionally took us out sailing in his own clinker-built gaff-rigged sailing boat which could take eight people. It was claimed he had sailed on one of Sir Thomas Lipton's J-Class 'Shamrocks' and still wore his white yacht crew sweater. I'm sure he thought this made him superior to the others in their ex-Navy regulation blue Guernseys.

For a tanner (six old pence) a week he 'kept an eye' on my father's boat at its mooring during the week, making sure she didn't sink. He was 'Captain' not from military service but from being a yacht skipper and he had a little finger missing. He'd caught it in a sheet winch years before. To us he was a hero. We boys chatted to them all and bought into all their stories of derring-do.

A wonderful photograph of these old boys appears on the front cover of a treasured little hardback book about Brightlingsea from my childhood. Called 'An Odd Cinque Port', it was written by L W (Len) Southern, a local personality I believe known to my grandmother. The book is undated but by deduction from the preface it was probably published in 1953. I don't know all the men pictured but Arthur Bowles is there in his white jersey. His footwear, white plimsolls

instead of boots, seemingly emphasised his status as a yachting man.

When we were kids and roaming these creeks, there were fishing and shrimping smacks working out of Brightlingsea and Wivenhoe. CK1 would leave before dawn for shrimping over the Swin sands and we would see them return soon after noon with the water kettle steaming away as if it were a steam ship, boiling up their tasty catch as they went. This, we knew, meant fresh shrimps for tea.

'CK' (for Colchester Creek) is the fishing authority code letters for the area. All fishing boat registrations around the country are two-letter abbreviations done this way. In the Swatchways, for instance, we have MN for Maldon, HH for Harwich and so on. At sea or visiting other ports, young (or even older) crew like to play the 'I-spy' challenge, guessing where vessels are from and registered. Privately owned and restored sailing smacks generally keep their numbers painted on the prow and on their sails. When we're away in another part of the country and see a 'CK' registration, emotive memories emerge. "Look, there's a Brightlingsea boat!" and the vessel is declared 'one of ours'. No doubt sailors from other home ports feel the same when they see boats with their two letters, regardless of who owns them now and where their current home might be.

The hard at Brightlingsea is spacious and more or less any size boat can be launched from here. There are often smacks and keel yachts on the scrubbing posts and upstream, on the other side of the yacht club jetty, is the Aldous Heritage Smack Dock of the Colne Smack Preservation Society. Established in 1971, it has led to many successful renovations.

Despite the closure of so many yards along the Colne up towards Colchester, the old boat-building skills haven't been lost for ever. Just a short walk from Brightlingsea hard, they are being taught again to young apprentices working under expert shipwrights at the Pioneer Sailing Trust base.

The Trust was formed in 1999 to restore the 'Pioneer', CK18, built at Rowhedge in 1864 and the last known example of a once large fleet dredging deep-sea oysters and scallops. Known as 1st Class Essex Skillingers, their name is a corruption of Terschelling, one of the Dutch Frisian Islands where they often fished. She was relaunched in 2003 and now has a full programme of sail training for young people and adults.

In its new building in Harker's Yard, the Trust has several other restoration projects on the go, including the 1870 Wivenhoe-built yacht 'Volante' and a Stour barge. A further construction dimension has been added to give pupils a taste of new-build experience and they also build to order a specially designed, 9ft plywood pram dinghy. On my last visit, they also had

The former Anchor Hotel and the 'mine' collecting box

a prototype, 24ft rowing gig, cold-moulded with three plies of veneer, to be used by local community-based rowing clubs for estuary racing, much like the clubs of Devon and Cornwall.

At the top of the hard is the shelter where the ferrymen and their cronies would sit yarning while waiting for a fare. There is also a bright red sea mine turned into a collecting box for Missions to Seafarers, quite common in our Swatchways ports.

The visually arresting former Anchor Hotel, now flats, but once the haunt of fishermen and the harbour master, is still much photographed, a familiar feature of the classic view of Brightlingsea waterfront. Colne Yacht Club, next to it, is not always open so, if necessary, walk a few yards up beside the shelter to the Yachtsman's Arms, still a traditional pub with an interesting local clientele. Serves good Greene King beers and pub grub.

If you have time and want to stretch your legs further, walk on by, up the road, via a little chicane into Colne Road and after a quarter of a mile at its junction with Station Road you come to the Railway Tavern. The line

The Railway Tavern

to Wivenhoe closed years ago. The station buildings were demolished and replaced by a community centre. But the old tavern survives to remind us of the line that used to be.

Quirky in the extreme and in a permanent state of modification or decoration, the pub boasts brewing on the premises in winter by master brewer Sarah. The brewhouse is one room, no bigger than a dining-room of the era – 1906, to be exact. The bar area not much more than a generous station waiting-room. Real ales feature as does a characterful, friendly clientele, locals rather than tourists. Open evenings only in the week but all day at weekends. No food. No inflated prices. Just an excellent pub for drinking with your mates.

From the Railway Tavern, you can take a bracing walk along the sea wall to Bateman's Tower, past a sea-water tidal-filled swimming pool, beach huts, café and other traditional seaside attractions. The tower is managed by Colne Yacht Club and used for its race starting line and also for the start and finish of the Colne Thames barge matches and Old Gaffers smack races.

Bateman's Tower, famous landmark and race line

Turn left out of the pub to reach the High Street, for shops, banks, a couple of other pubs and a church. The better known All Saints Church of Brightlingsea, dating back to the 12th century,

All Saints, the sailors' church

is about a mile or so up the single road that goes in and out of the town. On high ground, it is visible as a leading mark from the Colne Bar Buoy if you know what you are looking for. It is famous for the many plaques around the walls, memorials to local sailors and fishermen lost at sea since 1872, all historic maritime tales in themselves.

Brightlingsea has a fine maritime heritage but in modern times it is the many world-class dinghy (and catamaran) racers that has kept it a well known name in

Memorial plaques to those lost at sea

the sailing racing world. They come mainly through the town's second boating club, Brightlingsea Sailing Club, and include Bob Fisher, one of our kind contributors.

The clubhouse has a fine position on the Brightlingsea side of the creek, just ahead of the first houses and the main mooring piles. Get there on foot by turning left at the end of Waterside and walk between the sheds and past some town houses to find the substantial clubhouse. Once there, you have fine views across the creek and out to sea, not to mention the dinghy park and launching ramp. The race starting line stretches right across the creek to the Stone side so, if you arrive by boat when a race is about to start, expect to see the creek completely full, with dinghies jockeying for position and presenting a mass of sail to be negotiated.

The club runs the annual Pyefleet Race Week and regularly hosts open meetings for various classes. For these top-class events, races are started out in the river from committee boats but before and after racing the launching ramp is a constant colourful hive of activity.

In his 1953 book, 'An Odd Cinque Port', Len Southern said; "Brightlingsea Sailing Club is one of the up and coming clubs catering for the 'small man' of yachting, the man – and lady too, for the fair sex are becoming features of weekly racing at Brightlingsea – whose delight it is to race a boat of any size and any type, whether he is a proud owner of a boat, or able to borrow one for the occasion, or maybe is just a member of the crew."

Well, over the intervening 60 years the club has up and come, producing a string of both male and female dinghy world champions and scheduled to have its first lady commodore the year of publication of this book, 2012.

Brightlingsea's greatest claim to modern yachting fame lies in the development of world-beating catamarans in which the town's hero, the late Reg White MBE, played such a part. What's not on the board of honour is how much Reg, at the tender age of 16, contributed to the arrival of the 'new rig' for the Brightlingsea One Designs.

Raising the mast, shortening the boom and removing the little bowsprit gave the rig higher aspect ratio and a twin-spreader rig. It was an experiment that could have killed the class. It didn't. It raced and won mostly. The fleet is still going strong, more so than ever, with another 'new fangled' development, fibreglass hulls – Reg had one of the first off the production line. It's working for them, racing is keen and the boats, first designed in 1927 by Robbie Stone, are as pretty as ever.

Too long ashore! Time to get back to the boat and, with fresh fish and samphire aboard, head out to find a quiet night anchorage. Watch the sunset up the Pyefleet, maybe, and see where the river takes us in the morning.

Sunset over the Pyefleet

CHAPTER 9

Working the Colne tides

Up to Wivenhoe and Rowhedge, down and around to West Mersea and Tollesbury

East Mersea Stone, opposite Brightlingsea Creek, is a steep-to shingle point much favoured by smacks to run ashore and dry out for a scrub and bottom paint. Ease past Mersea Stone and the wreck of a wartime barge into Pyefleet Creek which makes Mersea Island an island. The creek goes as far as the Strood causeway that links Mersea to the mainland and can be covered at high tide. It is blissfully devoid of any housing development!

Glide in between bird-populated marshlands strewn with sea lavender to anchor in total peace at all tide stages. Mersea foreshore lies to the south but to the north there's nothing but open marshes leading to the slightly higher ground that is Fingringhoe, a couple of miles away.

The silence is enormous. Just the sound of waves lapping against the mud, which 'pops' as the tide recedes, and the distinctive chuckling ripple of the tide against the clinker-built planking of the many varieties of traditional boats that tend to frequent this tranquil anchorage. To the west, the spectacular sunsets over Colchester and the marshes must be some of the most photographed on the whole of the East Coast.

From here it's an easy passage to take the tide up the

Wivenhoe, barrier protected

Colne, destination the Anchor pub at Rowhedge for lunch, and take the ebb tide back. Turn to port at the Pyefleet red buoy opposite Bateman's Tower and pass the entrance to Arlesford Creek to starboard, where the railway bridge for the Brightlingsea-Wivenhoe line once was. Then, off Fingringhoe, the river begins to wind, with typical deep water on the outsides of the bends and shallows extending well out from the other side in classic meandering fashion. The north bank is well wooded here and this stretch is very pretty. You can see the old embanking that carried the trains following the line of the river.

Round another bend and there is the vista of the flood barrier, with Prior's Ballast Quay to port just before it, usually with a couple of barges loading.

To port is the entrance to Fingringhoe 'Roman River' Creek, where small coasters, assisted by a little tug, used to go to a tiny high-tide only mill quay. A friend's father was once skipper of such a coaster and was still squeezing in up the Roman River as recently as 1960. Now, though, the mill and warehouses are converted into smart flats and the river is no longer used.

The Colne was once an important route for shipping right up to Colchester's Hythe Quay and Brightlingsea, Wivenhoe and Rowhedge all had commercial wharfs on the way. Here ships and yachts were built and there were fishing fleets and timber-carrying ships in all these traditional Colne-side towns. Now, the former timber wharf at Wivenhoe is a smart housing estate and, when we visited, Rowhedge commercial wharf had signs announcing a similar plan there, too. The former yacht-building yard has already been housed over but it's rather an attractive place to live with its view across to the picturesque Wivenhoe waterfront. Here, too, the former Cooks Boatyard is also now a smart town- house development.

Cooks closed as a boatyard in 1986. Plaques on display on the quay around which the houses are built tell its history. One of the yard's last jobs was constructing the 55 metre steel hull for the Jubilee Sailing Trust's training ship 'Lord Nelson', the first ship to be especially designed for people with disabilities and wheelchairs. The Cooks closure meant she was moved at hull stage on to Southampton and then Cowes for final fitting out. A barque-rigged three-masted square rigger, she's a fine ship and an interesting part of Wivenhoe's part in our maritime heritage.

These days, just the J J Prior aggregates company keeps up the tradition of the Colne as a commercial waterway. More or less every tide, a J J Prior sand barge is to be seen motoring up or down river from the Prior sand works at Ballast Quay, Fingringhoe, on the west side of the Colne, just short of the Wivenhoe barrier.

Since 1934, the family has been extracting 'aggregates'

J J Prior's Ballast Quay, a distinctive part of the Wivenhoe boating scene

and loading their own barges with high-class sand and gravel destined for London via the Swin Spitway – hence 'Swin Rangers', the bargee's nickname for the Prior fleet – and up the Thames to Deptford Creek. They used to go to Fulham! It was done by sailing barge with just two crew. Now they are all motor barges with two crew and an engineer. But still, Monday to Friday, every tide regular as clockwork, one goes up the Thames, unloads and comes back on the very next tide.

The land access to Ballast Quay is via very narrow country lanes and no lorry access is possible. So the sea-borne method will continue until the sand runs out. Prior's says it is a lot more expensive than the road transport other Essex competitors use but they are maintaining a tradition and making their contribution to keeping road traffic down. An economic burden it may be but Prior sand has qualities that make it highly respected and much sought after. A great story of an iconic family operation that is still the salt of commercial life on the river.

The barrier at Wivenhoe was built just below the Cooks development primarily to protect Colchester from storm surge flood. It was prompted by the 1953 East Coast floods which damaged pretty much all of the Swatchways, from Canvey Island to Southwold. But it took until 1993 to be opened and operative. One of the by-products was a new site and clubhouse for Wivenhoe Sailing Club which moved from its former position on the town waterfront to just below the barrier. The move also safeguarded racing for the very pretty Wivenhoe One Design fleet which was able to moor off the new clubhouse.

The club members went to a lot of trouble to make sure the new building had an authentic Essex boatshed look and it does, looking long established and at home on the river bank. Another bonus was the addition of its own floating pontoon jetty out into the river and this little gem offers six free visitor berths with access two hours either side of high water. You need to be able to take the soft mud when the tide is gone. The club welcomes visitors but with no full-time staff is

Wivenhoe Sailing Club and jetty

not always open, so there is no booking in system. Just turn up on a first-come-first-served basis or make prior contact through the links on the club's website.

Part of the deal is that fishing boats can moor there temporarily. If the barrier is closed or at low tide they cannot get to their moorings so can stay for two hours. But a visiting yacht is likely to get alongside okay.

It is only a short walk up through the Cooks housing and past bijoux cottages with yacht berths opposite to the town waterfront and the splendid Rose & Crown waterfront pub. Situated on a corner, it has a very pleasant sitting out area right up to the river itself. Explore the roads leading upwards off the waterfront for more good pubs, shops and an interesting church, all adding up to one of the most attractive towns in the Swatchways.

The barrier is not often closed but, one of Prior's skippers told me, when it shuts it creates a backwash which makes turning their barges very tricky. "You have to turn them empty as there is never enough water room to turn them fully laden and, as we go off an hour or so after tide turn, we need to be facing the right way," he

Wivenhoe waterfront and the Rose & Crown

Ye Olde Albion

went on to explain.

Shoot the barrier (start the engine actually) and head on upstream. On the port side are moorings. To starboard is the picturesque quay with the pub and the colourful cottages much photographed and painted by artists. You continue round one more small bend to the grass-topped riverbank quays that are either side of the Anchor pub at Rowhedge, on the other side of the river. These are tidal, viable from two hours before to one-and-a-half hours after high tide, plenty of time for a beer and lunch, too.

On the upriver side of the pub is bank-side mooring space and a small floating jetty which can take small boats for a short time – a ferry runs from here to and from Wivenhoe – and then there are mud berth moorings beyond that.

Downstream of the pub is a dinghy launching ramp with a few dinghy mooring spaces, then another grassy quay. Here there are seats and pub tables linked to the alternative pub just over the road, Ye Olde Albion. This is a 'pub pub' with atmosphere, a friendly pub dog and

Alongside the grassy quay at Rowhedge

attractively priced good beers and no food other than crisps and nuts. But you can bring your own picnic to the outside tables if you are buying drinks from inside.

The Anchor offers a full restaurant menu for eating in the conservatory overlooking the river or in the patio area. When we paid a visit, we fancied the locally caught fish and devilled whitebait. Good beers and wines, too, but expect to pay restaurant rather than pub prices for a very agreeable experience.

The Anchor at Rowhedge

The quays and the surrounding houses are all beautifully clean and well maintained, obviously involving a lot of village community spirit. Several local boats were on the quay as well as visitors when we were there. The Warden can be summoned by phone and you can stay overnight for a small fee, as long as you can take the mud. Ropes ashore from the mast to prevent falling over are recommended.

There is a brief highwater stand and then the tide turns quite suddenly and for anyone not staying the night it is time to skidaddle!

In the afternoon, the south-easterly breeze tends to fill in and this, coupled with the ebb tide, usually results in an exhilarating short tacking duel with the meandering banks of the river. Sweeping onwards, you should soon be close fetching past Mersea Stone and Brightlingsea and on to the Bench Head buoy. Here, you can turn to starboard in safe water depth into the Blackwater and head for West Mersea, in time for evening sundowners.

West Mersea is a very popular sailing centre and yacht moorings are packed into all the entry creeks between the land, Cobmarsh Island, Sunken Island and Salcott Channel. A mooring place will be a distance from the landing jetty. There is a yacht club launch service but generally it's a fairly long dinghy ride in – outboard worthwhile.

Once this is solved, the landing is another typically low level dinghy jetty. It is now a floating one with a hammerhead and prominently signed as being not just for yachtsmen but a 'working jetty' for commercial fishing boats. Like Brightlingsea, it is another popular East Coast jetty for mass crabbing.

Popular spot – West Mersea town jetty

West Mersea is a town with a hinterland beyond the waterfront, attractive rather than picture-postcard as the old Wivenhoe waterfront is often deemed. The foreshore to either side of the jetty is full of boats and servicing sheds, including a slipway, and to seaward is flanked by a fascinating area designated for house-boats. Many have their own entry wooden boardwalks and have clearly been there some time. It was in these houseboat marshes that our contributor Richard

West Mersea houseboats

Matthews found the classic Fife yacht 'Kismet' to renovate, once it was no longer used as a houseboat – an unlikely vessel for such a purpose, anyway. Some of the others are sheds on floating pontoons rather than boats, but a few 'little ships' also live there.

West Mersea is blessed with the Dabchicks Sailing Club (100th anniversary in 2011) to one end of Coast Road which runs along the foreshore and the elegant and prestigious West Mersea Yacht Club at the other. The yacht club has a long history of members who have been prominent in local and international offshore racing as well as successful yacht designers.

Two good pubs to choose from: the Victoria, bistro-esque now, and the Coast, which in my young days was called the Social & Sailing Club. Revisiting it now, the bar area at least has hardly changed from how I remember it from 50 years ago. It also has a very friendly family feel to it.

West Mersea is a long established source of oysters, sent up to top London West End oyster bars and restaurants. The foreshore has two famous oyster 'sheds' to

The Company Shed – for fish to go or eat in

buy from and eat at.

The Company Shed has been there for 25 years and is fundamentally a wet fish shop, not limited to oysters, to buy to take home (open 0900 to 1700 but closed Mondays). You can also eat in the shop area itself (last orders 1600). A feature has always been to bring your own bread and wine, which is still the routine, but for a real local treat you can buy the white wines made at the Mersea Island Vineyard – what better to go with fresh local fish? Also on sale is a selection of local beers from the brewery based at the same vineyard. (The vineyard/brewery is midway across the island. Visitors are welcomed but it's a hike out of town or an hour's walk across from East Mersea Stone on the other side.)

The Shed has become a popular destination restaurant for people from miles around as well as sea-borne visitors. But there is no pre-booking so the advice is to get there early. Around normal lunchtime hours you might well have to queue a while. Be patient. It is well worth the experience.

The other option is to book at the West Mersea Oyster Bar, a few yards up the road. This is definitely a restaurant operation featuring oysters but with a full menu of fish and lobster, plus a wine list, and it is also a 'fish shop'. Open Sunday to Thursday 0900 to 1700, with hot food served 1200 to 1630, and on Fridays and Saturday open until 2200 with hot food 1200 to 2030. It, too, is very popular, especially with local residents, so best to book.

From the end of Coast Road, a splendid seawall country walk goes along the banks of Strood Channel. Eventually this channel reaches the Strood causeway to the mainland, thereby meeting up with Pyefleet Creek to complete Mersea's 'island' status. Once a year, an event that always gets a great turn-out of participants is the Round the Island dinghy race. It starts and finishes at the Dabchicks dinghy club but competitors can go whichever way round they choose. But crossing the Strood causeway has to be done by portage.

What with oysters and fish, pubs and clubs, Mersea wine and beer, boats to look at ashore and afloat, country walks and a town not far from the waterfront, no wonder West Mersea is such a popular home port for many boating enthusiasts. There are easy places to launch a trailed boat for anyone arriving by road for a short dip into the Swatchways. Just avoid approaching or leaving the island at high tide in case the Strood is covered over.

Before leaving Mersea Quarters completely, don't forget Tollesbury Creek, running up inside the Nass Sand, which can be explored when the tide is up. It has two channels, one north of Cob Island and one to the south which has more water. This creek becomes Woodrolfe Creek which is the access to Tollesbury

Tollesbury is famous for its wooden boat shipwright skills

Marina and foreshore which includes boatyards, a small wharf and mud berths. Tollesbury is a well known East Coast centre of shipwright excellence for fitting out and renovation work for smacks and traditional wooden craft.

While the rest of the creek dries out at low tide, the marina is kept at floating depth by a sill, so entry/exit is restricted to close to high water. At the entry to Woodrolfe Creek, a gauge indicates the depth of water over the sill. Do not pass unless there is enough for you! The marina has 250 berths and is pretty full, but some spaces are kept for visitors. Because of the tidal restrictions, this is not a come and go marina and once in you will need to dwell a while. No problem. Above the marina, on what counts as a hill in these parts, is the very attractive clubhouse of the Tollesbury Cruising Club.

Almost a country club, with a bar, restaurant, covered heated swimming-pool and tennis courts, the club welcomes visitors on an extended stay to enjoy the facilities. The elevated position provides a fine view

Boardwalk out to the berths at Tollesbury

The saltings sheds

from the terrace over the marina, the creeks and the marshes. The perfect place for an evening cocktail.

Alternatively, along the waterfront, you can swim in the public sea-water lido constructed in 1907, still popular and a safe play area for the kids. Beyond this is a fine row of saltings sheds, well preserved former yacht stores. Clapboard timbered and now painted cream with red roofs, they catch the eye and are frequently photographed. Hard by is Tollesbury Sailing Club, founded 1936 and, patronised by keen dinghy racers, still going strong.

Tollesbury village itself is a half-mile away. There are shops and a very attractive village square where you find the King's Head pub, a fine towered church said to date from 1086 and the ancient village lock-up, intended apparently for drunks to sober up in.

Tollesbury sits right in the centre of the Swatchways which seem to radiate out from it in all directions. This charming village encapsulates so much of the history and essence of these marshy, narrow and peaceful creeks, it is magic indeed!

CHAPTER 10

Voyages with the 'Maid'

No choice in the matter...Pyefleet to Burnham and a grandstand exit from Benfleet

Years ago, I once sailed with a character who would I am sure have had the nod of approval from Griffiths.

I first met Mike back in the 60s when he turned up one weekend, late in the season, sailing up the Crouch in a Northumberland Coble. He had read the stories by John Seymour who had sailed one of these rugged open boats to the Baltic. Mike was determined to follow, so he made his way to Amble on the Northumberland coast, about 25 miles north of Newcastle upon Tyne, bought a new wooden coble, then sailed it single-handed down the East Coast to Essex, a 300-mile or so passage.

Mike's Northumberland Coble

These sturdy boats were built to be launched from steep shingle beaches. But they would also sit upright when they took the ground.

With my own dinghy I sailed in company with Mike for a few forays out of Burnham while he prepared for his offshore adventure. At Christmas time we hiked in Yorkshire, just for the hell of it! Then, without fanfare, he was gone, eventually sailing as far as Norway, but that is a story for him to tell.

Eventually he returned to Burnham and, tired of sleeping under canvas, he sold the coble and went in search of a boat with a cabin. This is where I join in this yarn.

I was working in London at the time and Mike and I often met over a Guinness or two. "I've found a boat," he said one evening. "She's in a mud berth round the back of Mersea Island, east side up Pyefleet Creek. The tide will be right this Friday night and the owner can meet us there."

It was just assumed that I would come along to help bring her around to Burnham.

Did I mention that this was February? It was dark and I remember carefully following the wavering light from a torch as we trudged out over the saltings, the rising tide creeping in around us, typical of the descriptions in many of MG's stories. Eventually the darker outline of a boat emerged. The tide was just lifting her and we climbed aboard.

'Maid Marion' was her name and she was a Morcambe Bay Prawner, 26ft long, gaff-rigged with a long bowsprit, stooping headroom and no engine. Perfect!

Mike dealt with the change of ownership formalities, handed over a wad of cash and, with only a very brief run through, the happy vendor wished us well and fled into the night across the fast disappearing saltings. I had no idea if any insurance had been arranged. Actually, now I do have some idea – most likely none!

No time to sit and thaw out, we were soon back on deck gathering in muddy lines and pushing ourselves out into the stream. Not far away, cars were splashing their way across the Strood, the causeway to Mersea Island which was just covering at full tide.

Everything aboard was unfamiliar and we needed to get out of the mud berth if we were to sail away next day. We managed to clear the anchor, pushed and punted ourselves out into the stream, found a deep spot and dropped it.

Inside the cabin we coaxed the paraffin lamps into life and, although the headroom was to say the least limited, it felt like luxury compared with the canvas boat covers we were familiar with.

In the morning, a thick mist hid all signs of outside life. A compass was not on the inventory so we guessed that with the tide now flooding we were probably pointing seawards. Slowly the world emerged and a light westerly whisper got us underway, out into the Colne river, via Pyefleet Spit buoy with Bateman's Tower on the edge of Brightlingsea Creek just discernable.

Slowly we crept over the incoming tide. We were aboard a keelboat now, so no chance of lifting the plate and slipping along in the shallows out of the stream. We were not really sure of our draft but the Ray Sand (Rays'n) Channel would be the shortest way around to the Crouch, that is, if we could get over the watershed before the ebb set in. What would Maurice have done? His books revelled in these navigation dilemmas.

'Maid Marion'

'Maid Marion' was slowly letting us learn her tricks. We found more sails and figured out where to hoist them. We were covering the ground faster now, heeling a little for the first time, but the freshening breeze was steadily heading us. The Swatchways were testing us. We had sailed this stretch many times but having a keel below made us nervous. To be absolutely sure of enough water, we would have had to go the long way, running east to the deeper waters of the Swin Spitway and then face a long beat up to the Crouch. So we decided to chance it through the Rays'n.

We carried on. A length of line tied to a rowlock became our sounder. The Buxey Beacon slowly came on the beam and round to the quarter. The depth was steadily going down – the ebb was certainly running now. We could see a sail far ahead but probably in the deep waters of the River Crouch. The westerly seemed to be freshening or was it the shallow water that was kicking up a quarter wave to lap aboard over the lee deck? Advice was freely given about the proper way to swing a rowlock. We speculated on the draft of a

Morcambe Bay Prawner and figured it would have to be built to suit those notorious west-coast shallows. Would the 'Maid' take the ground and sit in a ladylike fashion?

Soundings came down to a nose to foot reading. We were tearing along now. Do we keep her heeled to reduce draft and risk driving hard aground or let her stand up and touch for sure? Mike was muttering quotes from Erskine Childers' book 'The Riddle of the Sands': "Oh, well," said Davis. "If you fancy a sit-down meal, there is nothing like running aground for it."

There seemed to be no end to the shallows and yet this area had the cheek to call itself a 'channel'. It is, however, a real 'swatchway' within the definition: 'a channel between or through sand banks'. The sail we had seen earlier was now much closer and clearly a yacht on the opposite tack, sailing towards us. With a tall racing rig she had to draw more than 'Maid Marion' did.

Like a brake being released, the 'Maid' started to break free of her quarter wave as we found the deep water of the Crouch. A few tacks later and we realised that she was not designed to beat efficiently to windward over a foul tide. We dropped the pick at Shore Ends to wait for the new flood up to Burnham

As the Crouch is an essential destination in our up-to-date record of sailing the Swatchways, part of the plan to get there involved taking 'Antiope' from the Thames and eventually to Fambridge for a winter lay-up. On the way, we pass close to Benfleet Creek which brings to mind another 'Maid Marion' yarn during the time Mike had her.

Back then, Friday nights at Benfleet Yacht Club, a former Trinity House lightship moored on the north side of the creek, near the railway station, required stamina and invariably meant a slow start to Saturday. Fitting out was hampered by the proximity of the clubhouse and, as the short winter working days stretched out and May approached, challenges were issued by other members in the bar. With the confidence of a beer or two and warmed by the gently glowing potbelly stove, it was easy to make rash declarations. The first Saturday in May seemed a reasonable date for the first voyage, to break out of the restricted tidal creek and cock a snook at the rest of the fleet still languishing in the saltings or mudberths alongside their wooden stagings.

Mike, another friend David and I rushed through the final fit-out. The appointed day arrived and, in the club-room below decks on the old lightship, the massive oak ribs and Norwegian pine planking did a very good job of dulling the shrill of wind in the rigging.

So it was that we found ourselves short-tacking in the narrow creek, the spring tide nearly full, with a deep reef in the main and a staysail set. The swing bridge carrying the only road access to Canvey Island barred our way. The right of passage from Benfleet to the sea had existed

Benfleet YC's former floating clubhouse

centuries before the bridge was built. Today we were following the requested practice of being underway in the proximity of the bridge and making our intentions clear to the bridge-keeper.

The plaintive blast from our tin horn only served to rouse a few members from the warmth of the bar to stand and watch from the lee of the old deckhouse. No one could have doubted our intentions. No sensible yachtsmen would be charging around in a very restricted stretch of water dressed like arctic explorers while the bar was still open. Our bluff had been called the night before and, after all, a fresh nor'wester would be a fair wind for a run down the Thames or over to the Swale. 'Maid Marion' was a craft built for the rigours of the Irish Sea.

Just when we thought that the firmly shut bridge would be our excuse to call the whole exercise off and retreat to the bar for a consoling pint, there was a flurry of activity ashore. Road barriers were lowered and we no longer had a choice in the matter. The 'Maid' had never been blessed with an engine so the past half-hour had pushed our nerves to the limit. More than once she had barely missed stays of other yachts and our bowsprit had swung close to at least one glossy fibreglass hull. Now timing was critical.

The lengthening queue of cars swelled our audience as the bridge started to swing. Should we make another turn to windward away up the creek or would the groaning structure lift clear enough for us to bear away and take a run at it? A sensitive modern hull could have been held up close to the wind or backed up smartly if it stalled. A more deliberate planned approach was required when sailing an old working boat.

A perfectly timed squall raced down the creek, the 'Maid' heeled, tucked her gunwhales under and with the mainsheet eased to the knot we made another lunge towards the clubhouse. There was no room left to tack. Mike had the tiller hard up against the coaming and our vessel, sensing the opportunity to escape to the open sea, slowly turned her bowsprit towards the widening gap.

She stood up and the staysail crashed across to windward, goosewinged. It was a case of time on distance now, as if we were making a run for an imaginary start line. There were also two chances of disaster. Running by the lee, a crash gybe would certainly spin us into a broach. On the other hand, clipping the bridge with our gaff would likely bring the whole rig down.

There was, of course, room to spare but at the time we just held on and hoped. The 'Maid' shot through the gap and by the time we relaxed the bridge was closing behind us.

Our destination had yet to be decided but the thought of a long run round the Maplins followed by a windward slog into the Colne or Crouch had little appeal. Emerging from the creek off Leigh-on-Sea, we could see sunlight on the Kent shore down to leeward. "How about a run over to Hollowshore and a pint in the Shipwright's?" suggested David.

No further prompting was needed. We were away with a fair wind down the creek and had escaped the clutches of another few weekends of fitting out until the tide served again. And the Shipwright's Arms at Faversham fulfilled its purpose more than adequately.

I wonder if the GRP sailors of today are missing out on the joy of scraping back layers of varnish and paint before trying to put it all back on in between springtime showers. But then a quick rub down with gel coat polish does extend the season, I suppose.

Benfleet Yacht Club is now a smart land-based clubhouse, opened in 1984, with hard standings for dinghies, bankside moorings that dry out at low tide and some swing mooring trots in the creek. On the other side of the creek, on the island itself, there is direct access out to the Thames, clear of the old swing bridge we challenged. The swing bridge swings no more and there is now a second road bridge across the creek. Progress or evolution – the club still flourishes.

Maurice Griffiths was not one to look forward to a pub at the end of a passage but he was known to venture across the estuary to Kent.

As we relive the 'Maid Marion' run, we too on 'Antiope' are making our passage down Thames, with a healthy ebb tide beneath us and the Crouch as the eventual destination. But the tide is on the turn and although 'Antiope' is a motorboat speed is not her forte. We are off Leigh-on-Sea and in the same waters as that windy spring day aboard 'Maid Marion'. Our choices, as then, are dictated by time, tide and the weather.

And we have the same dilemma. Do we push on for another few hours out to the Whitaker, perhaps arriving at dusk, or should we tuck into the Swale or Medway for the night? As before, the sunlight on the Kent hills and the Isle of Sheppey look inviting and, once again, the Medway wins the vote and we swung the wheel. Before long we are passing the wreck of the SS 'Richard Montgomery', a World War II Liberty ship. With the tide swirling through those rotting derricks, she is a stark reminder of war and a sight I remember from earlier ventures. Her high explosive cargo still aboard and too unstable to move, she remains a daily threat to the nearby residents of Sheerness.

The flood now under us and with the benefit of two engines, we are soon well into the Medway. Here it was that in 1667 Admiral de Ruyter sailed in from the Netherlands and caught the pride of the English fleet napping at Chatham. You have to admire the Dutchman's seamanship. He was the very same Admiral who arrived out of the mist and surprised the English before the Battle of Sole Bay off Southwold.

That evening we take up the kind invitation to spend the night on the pontoon of Rochester Cruising Club, a short walk from the old Dickensian town. There, I spot in an old ship chandler's window some ships biscuits displaying the sign, "If your crew complain of hunger, give them one of these. It will either cure the complaint or they will put up with the hunger."

CHAPTER 11

Aground on the road to nowhere

The Broomway, Paglesham and the Roach

We had dropped into Rochester Cruising Club up the Medway for our overnight on our trip from the Thames round to the Crouch and the Swatchways proper. Leaving the Medway early to catch the ebb tide, it's so still, no-one around but a barge setting her topsail, we are moved to keep our engines in tick-over so as not to break the spell.

I feel a touch of guilt pushing a button to set our next waypoint. Would Maurice have approved? Being old sailors and interested in the shape of our surroundings as a whole, we still like to look at a proper paper chart, too. MG would surely have agreed with that.

A barge under topsail creeps out silently ahead of us

We unfold the familiar 'Tilbury to North Foreland and Orfordness' chart, returning to my old stomping ground. I am convinced that every East Coast yachting clubhouse and waterside pub has a version of this chart on its walls somewhere and countless voyages have been hatched over an ale or two, with fingers tracing a course through the sands. Our first mark puts us in the bottom left-hand corner.

We are just off Leigh-on-Sea and the low line of the Essex shoreline lies ahead. The Maplins, Foulness, the mystical 'road to nowhere' and the stillness of the early morning all combine to prompt yet another yarn from our early Swatchways days. It was the time I sailed my newly acquired 14ft dinghy on my first proper voyage as skipper from Leigh-on-Sea to Burnham, via the Havengore cut-through.

I was still at school when I inherited a well used clinker dinghy from my elder brother and for a season I bailed most of the River Crouch from its bilges as various friends and I explored the river during the school holidays. Despite attempts to seal her up, the remedy was always short-lived.

My father eventually tired of propping up the fortunes of the Bostik company and took me in search of another dinghy. For £100 we found one with dry bilges. It was 'Jacandor', a Johnson & Jago 14 footer, lying on the foreshore at Leigh. With all future pocket money on hold, I became her owner and for the next few years this solid little craft would take me up every East Anglian creek in and beyond the Swatchways, far into the inland waterways and even to the Baltic.

My first task as the new skipper was to get her from Leigh to Burnham.

To Copenhagen with 'Jacandor', a long way from home

One Friday evening, a gullible schoolmate and I waded out and climbed aboard with the essentials for the voyage: a borrowed primus, the mandatory cans of baked beans, some sausages, the same Thames Estuary chart, torch and sleeping bags. How soft we have become with maturity! With shouted assistance from dad and the previous owner, we managed to set up the gaff rig, cast off from the trot and, as a final send-off, make a couple of passes of Leigh Sailing Club.

The plan was to take the tide down to Shoeburyness, sit on the mudflats until morning and then take the next tide through the Havengore and into the Roach, the back door to the Crouch and Burnham.

I remember clearly the sunset as we bore away towards the end of Southend pier, jutting a mile out into the Thames. The lights of ships steaming up to London seemed very close but I knew we were safe if we kept to the inshore shallows. The pierhead lights, which at first seemed never to get any closer in the dying breeze, soon began to take form and stride towards us. The now ebbing tide was sweeping us towards the pier supports.

We quickly learned how to row our new charge and eventually cleared the pierhead. I doubt if anyone above even noticed us but the lights and music soon faded behind us. In the blackness ahead, the Thames Estuary winked and flashed as far as one could see. It was a sight that has lodged in my memory as part of the magic.

We checked our progress on the chart with the torch and used a crude lead-line to follow the edge of the sands until, in the gloom, we found the outer end of the wartime barrage, a menacing row of piles running out from Shoeburyness to the low-tide line. Once passed, we gybed over in the slight land breeze that was now blowing out into the North Sea and headed inshore. Somewhere ahead I knew that the tide would strand us on the mudflats, but there was the nagging knowledge that this area had been a bombing range and I imagined our steel centreplate slicing into some rusting unexploded shell.

We were doing well, the dark thin line of Foulness shore becoming discernable ahead. The centreplate was now almost all the way up and through the tiller I could feel the rudder occasionally touching the mud. Then with a crunch we stopped dead.

There was no explosion and within a few minutes we were high and dry. 'Jacandor' appeared to be sitting comfortably on a ridge so, having rigged the mainsail tent-like over the boom, we lit the primus, cooked supper and crawled into sleeping bags. MG would surely have approved thus far.

At dawn we looked out on a flat landscape of mud, relieved only by a slight rise caused by a stony road running parallel to the shore. We were sitting right atop the Broomway, the ancient road to Foulness Island

The Broomway

and nowhere else. We ventured out on to the track, marked in places only by stakes or rocks above a thin layer of mud. Laid down centuries ago, this causeway was built up with stones over a matt of willow saplings and some of the wood was still visible. The journey out to the island must have been hazardous in the days of the horse and cart, working between the tides and not straying from the road.

Looking out towards the sea, the tideline was barely visible and yet within minutes we could see it advancing towards us. Soon afloat again and clear of the Broomway, we had the uncanny experience of meeting the tide coming from a gap in the shoreline, through the Havengore, the very stuff of Essex swatchway folklore. A line of withies led us in between the sea walls and ahead a very old steel lifting bridge barred our way.

A surprised bridge-keeper arrived on his bicycle to find a rare customer. A mere dinghy but with the right of passage in her favour. This short cut between the Thames and the Roach and Crouch had become little used since the heyday of sailing barge trade. I remember wondering then how much longer this passage would remain possible – the bridge was already well past its use-by date.

By the time we wriggled our way through the channels to the Crouch, the tide was again on the turn. Hardening sheets, we turned out of the Roach, testing 'Jacandor' on the wind for the first time. It was a stiff beat up the reach to Burnham where my parents were waiting to meet us as we arrived, no doubt with big grins on our faces.

This time, with 'Antiope', as we leave the Medway astern, it is not the day to take our motorboat over the Maplins. We would have to wait some hours for enough water so no short cut this time. Our route will have to be down and around the Whitaker, adding an extra 20 miles to the trip.

Nevertheless, we are still determined to complete the Havengore circuit again. Sure enough, another day, we come up the Roach from the Crouch and anchor for an overnight stay just downstream of the Paglesham moorings, planning to visit the Havengore Bridge from the other direction.

Shuttlewood Boatyard's long-standing shed

Being a cruising man, MG favoured anchoring in the lower Roach rather than the busy racing scene at Burnham. At weekends, the Roach right up to Potton Island often provides a helpful dog-leg for the yacht racing courses but in the evenings and the rest of the week it is quiet except for the birdsong. It has changed little over the years.

A couple of miles further up the river is Paglesham, renowned in East Coast folklore. The Shuttlewood Boatyard's big black shed still stands by the hard. Here, 100 years ago, sailing barges were built within its walls to a maximum length 84ft, which left only a foot spare inside the shed. This quiet anchorage once saw fleets of Thames barges waiting for fair winds to slip through the Havengore and take the short cut to the Thames. A depth gauge against the shed would tell the skippers when the rising tide gave them enough water over the Maplin sands.

It was here in Paglesham that 'HMS Beagle' spent her final years. Her five-year round-the-world voyage from 1832, under the command of Captain Robert Fitzroy, was made famous by the writings of Charles Darwin. She was reduced to a hulk and anchored in the stream to become a 'watch boat', home to the revenue men on the lookout for smugglers. The locals will tell you that her bones still lie in the mud along the foreshore, though the gossip that some of the timbers were used to construct local cottages seems entirely plausible.

There is no marina here so it's a row ashore in the old-fashioned way. You then work up a good thirst by walking from the boatyard the eight minutes up the lane to the Plough & Sail at Paglesham East End. Paglesham Church End is a mile away and has an interesting

12th century church, St Peter's, and the Punch Bowl pub. There is a small creek nearby but not effectively navigable and the pub is used not so much by sailors as country walkers and locals driving out for the restaurant. It also features a good Stilton cheese ploughman's.

The Plough & Sail is not actually on the waterfront but has been a favourite for years for many a Burnham sailor, a typical Essex 'country cottage' pub, easy to imagine as a smugglers haunt. The bar is traditional but there is now a classy restaurant, too. The gardens include a play area for children. The number 60 bus terminates right outside. Its route from Southend is defined by stops at several other pubs along the way, the Royal Oak at Stanbridge, the Anchor Inn, the Chequers at Canewdon and the Punch Bowl at Paglesham Church End – the means to a possible day of exploration out in the country without the drawbacks of a car!

Next day, being at anchor, we don't row ashore again to check the tide gauge but do our own calculations. The morning tide is just off neaps but will allow enough water for us to get through to the bridge and

The Plough & Sail, Paglesham

Havengore Bridge

back. With a close eye on the depth sounder, we creep around Potton Island, slipping quietly past a couple of yachts anchored in quiet isolation. A few twists in the channel and there is the new Havengore Bridge ahead of us. I am heartened by the fact that the passage has been preserved, even upgraded, to last a good few years to come.

If you travel by car today past Southend-on-Sea and Shoeburyness, you will come to Great Wakering. Turn right, past rows of slowly rotting railway carriages and a few warning signs from the Ministry of Defence, and there out in the wilderness the road climbs the sea wall at the aptly named Wakering Stairs. At low tide, get down the other side and out on to the sands and you are on the Broomway, the ancient road to Foulness and full circle from where 'Jacandor' had grounded all those years ago. Except for the new bridge, nothing much has changed there. It's as mystical as ever.

CHAPTER 12

King Canute's river

The Crouch – crowded but empty

Perhaps I chose the wrong day to revisit Burnham-on-Crouch with my son, a keen sailor born and bred on the wide green sparkling waters of Auckland's Waitemata harbour. This was February, midweek, low tide, cold and wet, and a biting wind greeted us on the waterfront. A handful of boats swung on the moorings but the yacht clubs on the shore and the town seemed deserted, the silence in the main street broken only by the chimes from the famous clock tower.

The historic clock tower in Burnham High Street

We sought refuge before a roaring fire in the Olde White Harte on the quay. From there, through the Georgian windows, you can survey the river and judge the wind and tide and decide to stay for another pint or brave the elements. Trying to explain the charm of sailing on the Crouch to a young Kiwi used to Waitemata was proving difficult. But we have had other Kiwi guests aboard who have found the experience fascinatingly different from home waters. A summer day and a good sunset help, of course.

It is a few years later and a lovely warm day when we make the passage to include in this book, going back into the Crouch to pick up at Shore Ends, roughly where 'Maid Marion' had dropped anchor to await the tide after her arrival via the Rays'n channel.

The river entrance is clear on our plotter and slowly reveals itself in real time. The short seas flatten as we pass the shingle bank at Shore Ends, such a fitting name. Seals lie on the sands. They used to be a rare sight. Now, there are many and seal-watching tripper boats, such as the 'Lady Essex III', come out at low tide, picking up passengers from Wallasea Marina and Burnham Town Quay. 'Lady Essex' is also the regular ferry service between Wallasea Island and Burnham Town Quay, very handy for walking and visitors on a day out.

From here, Shore Ends, the river runs straight for four miles up to Burnham, lined by high sea walls that

Burnham quayside

Junior racing over for the day

hide the seaward fringes of Essex. As it ever was, the wind comes on the nose. Maurice would probably have dropped the pick to wait for the tide or settled down for the beat up the river. We are spoilt by modern diesel engines and we make it to Burnham.

Ashore, we set about sitting outside the Olde White Harte, this time in the sunshine. With a pint in hand, it seems little has changed from the summers I remembered. It is a Wednesday evening, the tanned sails of the Squib fleet tack in light airs ever closer to the shore, dodging the ebb tide. Burnham has put on its best summer mantle.

A short stroll further up the sea wall there is an interesting museum on three levels in an old boat-building shed down beside the Crouch Yacht Club. You can learn much more than just the sailing heritage of the town there. Run by volunteers, it is devoted to the history of Burnham and the rest of the Dengie Hundred peninsula.

You can keep walking up the sea wall to get to Burnham Yacht Harbour marina. The road access is via Foundry Lane off Station Road and the museum tells us this was the site of thriving industry, where iron castings were made for plough shares through to grand piano frames for the Cunard liners. "You see, an iron-framed piano would stay in tune at sea," I was told. Of such is maritime heritage made.

Back aboard 'Antiope' we head upstream. Above the moorings the river takes its first bend and the magic begins.

This is where, in those seemingly endless days of summer, we used to venture in the little Royal Corinthian club scows. We were in our early teens at a time before girls made life more complicated!

At Cliff Reach, if the tide is right, you can take the dinghy to the beach to barbecue or explore behind Bridgemarsh Island, with its winding creeks and the drowned farm. The brick chimney is all that remains.

Out in the stream, a yellow racing mark bears the name Canewdon, The name always fascinated me and as kids we would imagine the place where King Canute tried to hold back the tide. There may be some truth in the legend. Canewdon village is on the south side of the Crouch, a sub-district of Rochford. Nearby Ashingdon Hill was certainly the scene of the fierce battle in 1016 between the Danes led by Canute and the more peaceable Saxons under Edmund Ironside. Canute won the day, later to become a popular king, and the church built in his name still stands close by.

Upstream from Cliff Reach, the Crouch winds gently between low hills. Beyond the bend at high tide, sails seem to float above the line of the seawall. Green hills and hedge-lined fields look the same as I remember.

As the moorings at Fambridge come into view, a glance at my watch followed by a mental speed and

Ferry Boat Inn, North Fambridge

distance calculation determines that we can make it in time for a pint at the Ferry Boat Inn, North Fambridge. A deep water pontoon on the north bank of the river now makes it easy to tie alongside and hop ashore to the pub. Perfectly kept guest ales are served to us by the same family that has run the pub since I was here last, probably 40 years ago. This was always a favourite destination if the tide suited and it has not changed. A great time warp and part of the enduring magic.

Upstream from the Fambridge moorings, Stowe creek was once my Amazon river when I explored it in the family dinghy. Now a ribbon of marina pontoons offers a delightful sheltered haven.

Further upstream you come to Hullbridge. Navigation starts to get tricky for sailing yachts and the river becomes the domain of motorboats. I can remember short-tacking my barge yacht 'Swan' all the way to Battlesbridge, the navigable limit of the river, the leeboards just touching the mud on the turns. Humbling to think that, under sail alone, Thames barges made this trip regularly.

Parts of the old Battlesbridge Tide Mill remain

Battlesbridge owes its name not to any great conflict but a Saxon landowner named 'Bataille'. Just upstream of the present bridge, parts of the old Battlesbridge Tide Mill remain, attached to a length of the old dam wall. On the north bank, the 'new' steam mill, built in 1896, is now the focal point of an antique and craft complex and popular visitor attraction. Across the road, the Barge Inn has its old white weatherboards but inside all is crisp and new, the old dark and yellow smoke-stained

Sculling home

Empty upriver Crouch

walls preserved now only in photographs.

The River Crouch grows on you. Many a sailing visitor may never venture above Burnham but there are sheltered spots to be found, somewhere to drop the pick or tie up alongside.

An hour or so by train from London's Liverpool Street station, Burnham is today a viable residential town for commuters. Arriving by car, along the B1010, you follow the notorious 'Burnham Bends', a series of right-angle turns around the farm fields. Bends like this are not unique to Burnham. Visit Paglesham, Hullbridge, Tollesbury or Heybridge by road and you will find the same sort of bends in series. They are an Essex countryside feature, a piece of geographical history which illustrates how enclosing the land into fields progressed over the centuries.

For our Swatchways journey, it is now time to head back to the Blackwater by way of the Rays'n channel again.

We return down the river past the Burnham waterfront. There is a natural limit to the mooring space in

Escaping upstream

this narrow river and the trots of one designs and keel boats each reflect the character of the various clubs they moor in front of. Offshore racers, Dragons, Squibs and so on from the Burnham Sailing Club, the almost adjacent Crouch Yacht Club, the Royal Burnham Yacht Club and, last downstream, the Royal Corinthian Yacht Club.

Most clubs are traditional buildings befitting this traditional, unchanged waterfront with its many old cottages and pubs. But one stands out. The Royal Corinthian (RCYC) is a distinctive concrete cube which was very avant-garde when it opened in 1931. Some hate it, many more photograph it, but it is always a welcoming landmark when returning home to the Crouch.

Going further downstream of the RCYC, we come to the Rice & Cole moorings, the unofficial home of the Narrow Seas Club – but no clubhouse. This once men-only cruising club was set up as a breakaway from the Little Ship Club, London, once it decided to allow lady members. The Narrow Seas Club eventually also survived the introduction of female members and is still thriving. I joined in my teens when the members met in a London pub to plan their season's cruising, The Swatchways are still their territory, the club's white gull burgee a common sight along this coast.

The river gives us a smooth run down to Shore Ends. Seals, our only company, lift their heads o watch us pass. They're probably fishing now. At low tide they will be basking on the banks. As the river widens, we edge to the north, looking for a comfortable, safe, contour line on the sounder. Finding our way through this time, even with the aid of a chart plotter and echo sounder, seems just as testing as our voyage had been coming the other way in 'Maid Marion', the Morcambe Bay Prawner.

The Dengie Flats to port become just a dark horizon line, only broken by a few trees. The Rays'n channel is still no more than a slightly deeper bit of the Buxey Sands. We are looking out for the ancient chapel of St Peter-on-the Wall as a sign that we are nearly through.

Yes, there it is, a simple chapel dating from 650 AD, sunlight reflected from its red-tiled roof. Further on, the mass of the Bradwell Power Station dominates the entrance to the Blackwater. As the flat sands slowly give way to deeper water, we turn to port into the Blackwater to return to Maldon again.

St Peter-on-the Wall, Bradwell

CHAPTER 13

A winter's sail

On board a Gunfleet 43 in the Orwell

The Gunfleet 43

Officially, it seems, 'winter' is December to March so mid November for a late-season sail still counts as 'autumn' – even if most of us think anything after the clocks go back is most definitely 'winter'. In the third week of November, we set about taking advantage of a weather window for a couple of days' cruising in the Orwell before winter proper sets in.

MG wrote about winter sailing in February which was a rugged affair, trying to keep warm with ever more layers of sweaters and jackets and real wax-coated 'oilskin' coats. These days there are many autumn and winter racing series which have greatly extended the use of boats beyond traditional laying-up dates, made all the more enjoyable by modern clothing technology designed to keep warmth in and cold water out. Plus, it must be said, modern materials for ropes and sails make sail handling considerably easier than the old three-strand hemp and canvas. Clubs organise races, usually at weekends, and take the weather as it comes.

The pleasure for the cruising sailor is to do his winter sailing in his own time, when a happy combination of sunshine and light winds occurs and the river is empty of moored boats or a racing fleet. You get much more of a sense of space and tranquillity because the colder, heavier air dampens sound in general but at the same time makes certain sounds more audible, those normally drowned out by the noise and chatter of summer-time crowds.

For this mini cruise we are sailing a brand new boat, the Gunfleet 43, built by the Colchester-based Gunfleet Marine, Richard Matthews' second and most recent boatbuilding enterprise. It's a great opportunity to compare over a spectrum of 80 years what a modern cruiser can offer versus the boats which MG sailed in the original book.

The Gunfleet Sands are deeply embedded in an East Coaster's psyche, in folklore and first-hand experiences. A few miles offshore from Clacton and running south-west to north-east from the Crouch to Harwich, in a way they define the offshore limits of what we call the Swatchways. These emotive sands which feature in many a sailing-barge story or shanty are now at the forefront of technical revolution as the site of an offshore wind farm. Forty-eight turbines stand out against the horizon like giant white plants brought by aliens from outer space, with three uniform 'leaves' whirring away on top. Some people hate them. Others like their statuesque symmetry. Spot them and you know where you are on the water.

The sands are to be avoided in rough weather. But, linking with the Buxey Sands at the southern end, they create a sheltering breakwater effect from rough seas whipped up by strong south-easterly winds on the coastal passage from the Blackwater to Harwich and the Stour and Orwell rivers.

We join the boat just before noon at Fox's Marina, Ipswich, Gunfleet's operational sailing base. We quickly ease out into the river and hoist the main in the reach below Ipswich docks, with the spans of the Orwell Bridge just below us. Killing the engine, we bear away and unroll the jib. Despite only a light Force 2 breeze, we are off like the Manningtree Express.

The air feels 'clean' and, as we beat down the winding river, the press of the wind on the sails in the frequent little freeing gusts seems more exaggerated than you would expect in the summer.

The river scenery is peaceful. With hardly any boats left out on the moorings, we think what their owners are missing, having laid up already – too soon as it has turned out this particular year. The whole vista of the river is empty and we muse that this is close to what the river must have looked like at the time of MG's book.

A winter sail in warm enough temperatures really is magical, partly because it shouldn't be so good at this time of year and partly because it feels like a stolen day, especially if you can sneak away on a weekday at short notice, as we did. Wicked!

The weather forecast had dictated our date to sail rather than the tide tables and it just so happens that the tide is against us, flooding. The passage plan is open but the general idea is to get to Harwich or even Mistley for lunch.

We are only three on board, skipper Mathew, Anneliese (Anna), both less than half my age, and myself, but the boat is set up for short-handed sailing, everything easy to work from the centre cockpit. The roller furling jib and effective lazy jacks to handle the main seem to an old romantic like me very akin to the brailing up method in the sail plan as it developed for the short-handed sailing of old working Thames barges.

Aboard a modern family cruiser, the latest in easy sailing and creature comfort, one can afford to dream and relate to the 'good old days' of flax, hemp and canvas. MG described quite a lot of winter sailing and although he obviously revelled in it I am sure he would have liked the warmth and dryness of today's boats. His boats seemed always to be leaking somewhere and the stove below and hot brews were the main saving grace.

The boat sails beautifully and close to the wind, tacking made effortless with the short-footed jib in the sail plan and the luxury, for a boat of this size, of push-button electric winches. We are often able to hold a course in the slightly shifty breeze close along the line of empty mooring buoys. Managing six knots and nearly out of the tide, we make good progress down river, with extra shelter from the slight bite in the north-easterly from the generous cruising spray dodger which we sensibly keep in place. The high centre-cockpit steering position of the Gunfleet 43 affords marvellous views to port and starboard as we sail along.

Good views from the high centre cockpit

It feels as though we are deep into the countryside. Most of the fields behind the sea walls are pastures and, if you are not sailing, horse riding seems to be the thing hereabouts. The quiet and emptiness are so beautiful that, even against the wind, the sound of workmen strimming the river banks comes across as strident, intrusive even. But we have to accept this as rural, seasonal background noise.

We beat on down past Levington. Ahead loom the giraffe cranes on Felixstowe Docks that we had spied from our Walton Backwaters trip, looking quite grim in the grey-scale light. They are working away at a couple of container ships which blanket our wind for a while but the Gunfleet sails on quite happily in the wind hole, still making over the tide in next to nothing. Then we are clear of the ships and once Shotley Point is to starboard we can bear away to reach up the Stour towards Mistley and Manningtree.

Mistley Marine & Leisure Ltd dock is where many of the racing Thames barges come at the end of the annual Barge Passage Match from Gravesend to Shotley

(Harwich). I took part in it a few years ago without any racing distinction but the raft-up there at the end with all the other competitors was terrific. Shore barbecue set up by team supporters, beers and barge chat and all of us, naturally, still in our slightly grubby sweaters and Caterpillar boots.

But limited daylight hours means that Mistley will have to wait for another day. We round up to drop the sails, the roll-up jib and the smooth running of the main into the jackstays making the job easy. We moor up alongside the Harwich Halfpenny Pier visitors' area, empty on such a day.

When we had visited in the summer, it was very popular inside and out and clearly a favourite first port of call for Dutch and Belgian yachts come to cruise here. Anna, coming originally from Holland, feels almost close to home. She lives for now in another classic Swatchways town and normally sails on a local smack. The Gunfleet is quite a change for her, wheel steering a first for a start. She is much impressed with a boat that is so easily driven through the water. The old gaffers are

Alongside Halfpenny Pier

pretty and a traditional sailing experience but there is nothing like sailing a fast and easy cruising boat for the fun of just getting there.

And here we are on Halfpenny Pier. Snug alongside, we head for the Pier Hotel for a light lunch. This historic hotel was known for its connection to the Navy yards and the original ferry traffic (now moved up the river to Parkeston Quay).

When we first started offshore sailing on 'Evenlode' out of Burnham, the great feature race of the season was the Harwich-Hook (now called the North Sea Race, with the finish line moved to Scheveningen). Taking part in a Royal Ocean Racing Club (RORC) race with a foreign destination was a significant step up for us young novice offshore crews and approached with great respect and excitement. An 'international' fleet, too, attracting entries from the Continent.

I remember two Dutch boats in particular. One was the powerful cutter-rigged 'Zwerver', winner of the race in 1960 and '61. At nearly 57ft. she was the biggest in the fleet – maybe not so big by today's standards – powering her way to lead the fleet out of the harbour.

The other was 'Tonnerre de Breskens' owned and skippered by Piet Vroon from Breskens in the Netherlands. As I reminisce now in front of the Pier Hotel about my first North Sea Race in 1962, Piet Vroon is still offshore racing somewhere on the international scene with his latest 'Tonnerre' – and still winning. Our friendship developed from those early East Coast encounters and when we meet now the talk may be of the latest hot-shot racing but memories of our East Coast racing roots and social events like the Medusa Club rallies are never far away.

To sail in such company made us youngsters feel very macho and crewing in the race officially counted as experience towards qualifying for eventual RORC membership. I am happy to be back now where it all began and find very little changed.

The Pier Hotel was the starting box for the race, the race office and flag poles installed on the first-floor balcony. The course in the direction of the Deane buoy was constrained by channel buoys so a reaching start was quite usual. We would set off in a flurry of sails, foam and shouts for 'water' and 'Zwerver' would soon be ahead, seemingly regardless of where she had started. A bit of a mêlée around the Guard Buoy and then we were free for our passage to Holland and our first lessons in the art of drinking Dutch beer with Bokma gin chasers.

For me, this is still one of the attractions of cruising in the Netherlands. Many East Coast sailors evidently think so, too, enough for the East Anglian Offshore Racing Association to hold its annual EAORA Week regatta over there, usually around the end of June. You can join in with the 'week' or any of the other 10 or so races the EAORA organises every season. One of the positive aims of the association is to make the process of joining in its programme as simple as possible.

Back to the Swatchways and the present. Not many people around on Harwich quay. A lifeboat arrives at the RNLI station on the quay, flamboyantly reversing into its dedicated dock after an exercise, it seems, rather than a serious rescue. The station has an interesting exhibition room which we visited last time in Harwich. This time, we cross over the empty road and take a table in the window of the Pier Hotel's Ha'penny Bistro. With wooden floors and tables, it's pleasantly

The Pier Hotel

warm and has views of any activity taking place on the quay. The menu, not too complicated and all cooked to order, includes locally caught skate wings which are snapped up quickly, plus bistro-style brochettes. With a glass of Greene King IPA bitter on the side, it is all very civilised and a true autumnal pleasure.

But daylight is going and we need to get a move on. The tide has turned so we will be against it but, this time, broad reaching, we make excellent and direct progress close to the mooring buoys and as far out of the tide as we can. Ships come up regularly to Ipswich and the main channel is deep enough but once you get among the mooring buoys the depth drops very quickly. Best to run alongside and not inside of them.

The 'cooked to order' at the Pier Hotel had made us linger a little longer than intended and dusk arrives quickly, due to the cloud cover. The channel buoys are all lit but the river wiggles and you have to make sure you have the lights in your sight in the correct sequence. The bends mean that sometimes you can get it wrong and what you think is the next one isn't!

Fortunately, the Gunfleet has a very easy to read, 12in screen, chart plotter to follow and confirm your course. This is mounted on a cleverly designed pedestal known as the Flightdeck® and exclusively developed for Gunfleet yachts. The steering wheel is mounted on the front side and curves towards the helmsman, surrounding the pedestal like a saucer on its side. Thus the spokes of the wheel are kept clear of the plotter screen and the instrument button controls.

As night falls the wind dies on us, as often happens in the summer, too. We furl the sails in a trice and the iron mate is instantly active at the touch of a button. Very silent, controls conveniently all on the Flightdeck® pedestal, she is delivering eight knots plus at only 2000 revs, a very handy speed for cruising.

In the darkness, the river seems even more empty and quiet. MG would have enjoyed the river at this time of year.

Soon Pin Mill comes abeam to port. The very bright fluorescent orange/yellow floodlight on the Butt & Oyster pub seems to be urgently beckoning us ashore, like the light of the Cornish wreckers (a myth, they now say). Tempting, but we have to press on.

We line ourselves up with Orwell Bridge and pop through, only to be confronted suddenly by a coaster hauling off the dock to head downstream. The tide has been ebbing a while so we are a bit surprised she is leaving now but we assume the pilot knows what he is doing and there's enough water for him to go. As we slow a bit to let her crab across our track to the correct downstream side of the fairway, we squeeze to starboard close to a remaining ship on the dock to pass port to port. As soon as we clear the ship's stern, we are right up to the entry to Fox's Marina.

It is quiet and dark. Lights are twinkling on shore buildings and a few occupied boats in the marina berths and it feels like a real homecoming as we slip almost silently into the berth. A delightful, comfortable but simple cruising yacht as modern as we could get has given us another magical day out.

Commissioned by Richard Matthews to a design by Tony Castro, built in Colchester and fitted out at Fox's of Ipswich, the Gunfleet 43 could well become the new iconic yacht of Essex and Suffolk. More Gunfleet models are planned. At the time of our sail a 58ft was already in build and a 70 footer definitely on the cards.

From a cruising point of view, what appeals is the easy to handle sail plan, spacious centre cockpit, wide after deck for sunbathing and copious but uncomplicated living below decks. MG could never have known such luxury. We wished he could have been with us to see it.

CHAPTER 14

Magic carpet for charter

No boat? No worries!

The bright, autumnal day arrives as predicted, with a clear blue sunrise, pale and gentle, and very pleasant temperatures to come later. Ideal for sampling a Swatchways charter sail.

Chartering, a yachty word for renting, is a very convenient, cost-effective alternative for finding the magic. There was nothing like it available to MG in 1932. To charter opens up great possibilities for both novices or experienced sailors, especially if you are not sure about bringing your boat from another part of the coast or simply do not have a boat at all. If you have already laid up a boat on a pre-booked date and then find an Indian summer kicks in, a day charter is the route to a bonus extra day afloat, as it is for us.

For the experienced, the usual options are bare boat, the term used for self-drive with your own crew – although the boat itself will be anything but bare of equipment – or skippered, usually with one professional skipper and up to five of your crew. It's the ideal way to guide a newcomer to the Swatchways to the best places for a weekend, a week or more.

Without our own boat here any more, 'Antiope' now in the Netherlands, I contacted the East Anglian Sea School, a local charter operation, to fix a short winter sail. It was arranged at short notice when the forward weather forecast looked good and I arrive sharp on time at the EASS offices in the marina of Suffolk Yacht Harbour, Levington, on the River Orwell. In late November, the autumn sun is quite low in the sky but there is enough warmth in it for sailing in just a light jacket.

The school was founded on the Blackwater in 1973, the same year the RYA (Royal Yachting Association) began its training schemes. Now owned by the second generation of the same family, it offers all the official RYA courses. But, above all, this is a very friendly school and, under principal Peter Smith's direction, the focus is heavily on 'recreational sailing'. Exactly what I'm looking for – a gentle winter's sail purely for the interest and sheer pleasure of it.

The point of the school's particular philosophy is either to get people afloat for the first time or to get them confident and competent in their own boats so they can make more of their investment without a plethora of tests, forms and paperwork. In the season, courses are available on the live-aboard offshore yachts or five-day residential courses in dinghies are run for kids or adults who are accommodated in bed and breakfasts in the area. There are charter boats for racing, too – even to participate in the sometimes intrepid Fastnet Race down south – but our concern for now is cruising the Swatchways and here the EASS excels. It is their back-yard, after all, offering a cruising area from Lowestoft to Ramsgate and is based right in between them on the Orwell.

With the minimum of formalities, within 10 minutes of arriving we are aboard 'Strata 3', one of the school's

Silvery winter sunshine

reliable Jeanneau 36s, well equipped, all in perfect order and clean and fresh down below.

We slip out of the silvery still waters of the marina into the river. We find the same north-east wind gently blowing as I'd had on the Gunfleet 43 sail but this time with sunshine dominant and only a few high clouds about. Sails are hoisted and, with Peter and Andy from the school crewing, making us just three aboard, we turn upriver with the wind astern and the jib goose-winged on the very easily rigged spinnaker pole. It is a cruising roller-furl high-cut jib giving good visibility underneath it.

Once again, we are sailing in a near deserted river. A couple of late season cruisers are out for a bit of rig tuning and a coaster comes by en-route to Ipswich docks. But otherwise the whole world is gripped in a cool, calm stabilising atmosphere.

Winter sailing can be some of the most pleasurable. In my racing days, we once went out for some friendly self-arranged fun racing round a short Solent course on a Saturday in December, with a late lunch in the club-

Butterman's buoy

house the prize. The sun shone and we raced as hard as usual in flat winter water but with a nice Force 3 blowing. Winter wind is heavier than the summer equivalent and winch-winding was hard work, the crew doing their stuff in T shirts.

The race was done, someone won and after the lunch we returned to London, the boat due for laying up the very next week. Saturday night in London passed and we woke up Sunday morning to four inches of snow on the ground and T shirts were replaced by full winter coats. That's the chance you take with winter sailing so grab the sunny days when you can.

With the tide under us, we soon wriggle our way around the channel to arrive at Butterman's Reach, just out from the hard at Pin Mill. This gives rise to a discussion as to whether the Butt & Oyster pub is named 'Butt' after Butterman's Reach or vice-versa, or after a butt of wine or beer, a barrel of about 100 gallons capacity. Such conjecture is only possible on a peaceful day with harmonious people in relaxed mode. The 'oyster' to go with the butt would have been harvested locally, we all agree with satisfaction, our mouths silently watering at the thought.

The pub has been there since the 17th century and can be reached by road turning off the B1456 from Woolverston at the signpost to Pin Mill at the village of Chelmondiston. The lane is narrow, but there is a

Pin Mill and the Butt & Oyster beckon

car-park area down in the hamlet itself and a few spaces for customers round the back of the pub. A pretty place, much photographed and painted.

Another pub, the Turk's Head at Hasketon village near Woodbridge, prompts a new discussion because its sign sports the turbanned head of a Turkishman. This fine local country pub is near enough to the Woodbridge maritime scene for the locals to say the name comes from the Turk's Head knot and that, they maintain, is what should be on the sign, not a man at all.

The Butt beckons but we resist again, partly because we need a dinghy to get ashore – the EASS will provide one if requested but we don't have one on board today. 'Strata 3' is kept in commission all winter so maybe another sunny winter's day will arise when we can plan a passage, making the Butt & Oyster the lunch destination and bringing along a dinghy.

The beat back is against the flood but even in this light Force 2 the boat sails well with the cruising jib. We stick to the main channel as, the minute you go beyond the line of empty mooring buoys, the mud comes up quickly and tacking depth is no more than a boat's length beyond. In the summer the buoys are full of yachts with hardly a gap between them, so people usually stick to the channel anyway.

The sun is shining strongly, keeping us all comfortably warm. It is so low in the sky the reflection of sunlight on the river is elongated and an intriguing silver-white, contrasting with the deep winter green of the grassy sea wall. It seems to shine below the surface of the water rather than upon it, like a summer sun does. Is this all part of the winter magic?

An Oyster 80 under engine comes by from Fox's Marina, the Oyster base at the top of the Orwell, crossing ahead of us as we tack over, kicking up a wash made more noticeable by the still winter water. No clue as to where she is heading with a crew of four on board. Surely it's too early for exhibiting at the London Boat Show in January but she may be leaving for a transatlantic delivery to the Caribbean.

Part of the romance of sailing, when you see a boat leaving port and heading out to sea, free of the ties of the land, is to wonder where she is bound – perchance to dream of being with her! The anticipation of winter at home probably prompts such thoughts. Meantime, we are sailing contentedly to our own destination which, having now had our time, is back to base at Levington.

The jib is rolled away and the main dropped and given a fold stow as we glide into the marina. Some famous boats live here, such as 'Undina', a beautiful restoration, and 'Fanfare', a Holman & Pye timber hull, one-off design built for the 1965 Admiral's Cup race series. I had crewed on her the year after. Then she was a Class I 'big boat' but now looks quite small against some of the voluminous modern creations. She has a distinctive kicked-up transom, a design result of the rating rule of the day, and I recognise her instantly, even though she is painted light blue now rather than the original white.

'Fanfare' is over 50ft but our 36-footer seems to have higher freeboard and appears almost as big. I bet we have the same amount of bunk and galley space!

Even at this time of year, the marina is virtually full of winterised boats with a few, like our EASS yacht, still in commission. Ashore there must be a hundred more laid up. No wonder the river looks empty...they are all in the fields above.

Now comes the best part of charter sailing. The berth is reserved for our 'Strata 3, the mooring lines ready there on the dock. Tied up, we have a few moments to sit and savour the stillness. Then we hop on to the floating pontoon to go ashore and that is that. The EASS crew takes charge and the charterer has nothing more to worry about. It's a great way to enjoy the Swatchways, especially for anyone new to them. It's the simple, no-worries approach to getting afloat.

'Strata 3' in her marina berth

As planned, we repair to the Haven Ports Yacht Club's bright red lightship moored on the inner pontoon to chat a bit more about the charter option.

One of the EASS's specialties is own-boat tuition, whatever the vessel. How to handle sailing yachts or dinghies, power boats, sports boats or RIBs can all be taught in a recreational boating way or you can take an RYA certificate course if you want to.

The mainstay of the school, though, is instruction using boats in its own fleet. They have three Jeanneau 36s, a RIB, a Haines twin-screw motor cruiser, Wayfarer dinghies for adults and a fleet of Feva dinghies for teaching youngsters while their parents do their own thing. If you really want to get away from the English weather, the school has another arm in Turkey, the East Aegean Sea School, with boats for charter.

For now, though, we are sticking to the Swatchways, full of relatively easy sailing and loads of places to visit. Accessing the magic at a time to suit you with no fit out and launch logistics to arrange is only a phone call away to a charter company!

The yacht club is inevitably ship-like, cosy and warm, with a fully stocked bar and offering tasty food for lunch or supper. The lower-deck function room is perfect for a crew party.

There is no need to go any further but the 13th century Ship Inn is just a 10-minute walk up the lane in Levington village itself. We'd had supper there the night before. With beams and flag stones and run by independent owners, the Ship is a real biscuit-tin country pub serving the full range of Adnams ales – also a decent, not too expensive house Shiraz. At this time of year, a substantial iron stove is roaring away and the excellent

Winter sailors returning home

seasonal menu includes local partridge.

The substantial, brick-built, towered church next door is another St Peter's. The choir came into the pub the night we were there after choir practice, a lovely village touch, we thought. Near to but not on the waterfront, the Ship has a wide sweep of open views over the meadows down to the Orwell, where you see horses trotting by rather than sailing boats. Very busy in general at weekends in the summer but in the winter and around spring fitting-out time the pub is very popular with boaters up from the marina.

Lightship lunch done, my charter taster is now really over. The sun shone, the wind was gentle, the boat and the company a perfect match for the day out and, for me, nothing more on 'Strata 3' to worry about. Job done. Magic!

CHAPTER 15

Growing up the East Coast way

Richard Matthews tells how the magic began for him – and continues

When it comes to the 'your favourite places' question, a lot of grown-ups will click back to their childhood memories and this kid is no exception.

My dad and I learnt to sail at the same time in the creeks of West Mersea with Ed Wyatt, the proprietor of the local boatyard, in 'Chum' a 14ft gunter-rigged traditional clinker dinghy. My dad and Ed Wyatt are in the clouds now and I'm sure 'Chum' is long gone, but the embers of those early skills, learnt at the age of four or five, are still glowing.

Richard aboard 'Kismet' in 2011

I was chatting with Russell Coutts on the quayside in Plymouth recently. Russell is arguably the world's top racing sailor and I was flattered to be able to remind him that I'd beaten him twice in 12 Metre World Championship races. Those early years racing in the handicap fleet in the creeks and estuaries of

A favourite pose since childhood!

the East Coast were not wasted.

My first boat was a pram dinghy given to me by my dad. It was pretty rotten but I rigged up a sail made from a bed sheet. Half-an-hour's row upwind was followed by the pure joy of 10 minutes downwind, steered by an oar. Next came 'Dumbo', a Yachting World pram built by dad, with a dagger board, rudder and real sails. The sail in this case was cut down from a World War II airborne lifeboat sail, which matched my World War II 'V for Victory' kapok lifejacket. 'Dumbo' could go to windward so this was 'real' sailing and the freedom for an eight- or nine-year-old kid to stay afloat from dawn to dusk and explore every inch of those Mersea creeks.

Then came 'Swallow', a lovely 12ft lugsail dinghy with bamboo spars and a heavy iron centreboard. She sailed like a witch and I won a silver cup for runner-up cadets' points racing with the Dabchicks Sailing Club. 'Swallow' leaked like a sieve and twisted so she would sail heeled at the bow and upright at the stern but that trophy is still among my most prized possessions.

Peter Bowler was a Mersea character and the day before he left to work in the USA he sold me 'Teal' for the princely sum of £45. 'Teal' was a 21ft half-decked gaff-rigged keelboat from about 1890. She needed some work to get her back in commission, including

"Then came 'Swallow', a lovely 12ft lugsail dinghy"

re-covering the deck and full length copper tingles over her decaying garboard planks, with a whole tin of black mastic roofing compound each side to keep the water out. 'Teal', with her lead keel and balanced rudder, looked and sailed like a real yacht. She was seaworthy enough to sail anywhere within the Blackwater Estuary and with her protected cockpit, free from an intrusive centreboard case, she was every girlfriend's favourite day out.

We were precocious little beggars in those days (and probably still are). I remember one windy day, when the local cadet week racing was cancelled, we sailed 'Teal' four miles out of the Blackwater and around the Bench Head buoy just to show we could. In those days we used to scour boatyard dumps to find half-used tins of paint or varnish we could re-use.

On one such search I came across the broken alloy mast from Reg White's original 'Hellcat', which he raced in the Little America's Cup. Reg sold me the stump for 10 shillings (a lot then but 50p in today's money) and that winter we re-rigged 'Teal' as a masthead sloop. Kim

Holman, the designer of the day, said she looked like a little ocean racer – we liked that. I can remember racing in Maldon one day, then sailing through the night to race at Wivenhoe next morning.

Meanwhile, father Bob had owned a couple of small cruising yachts including 'Sandora', a Lynette class four tonner that we sailed all over the East Coast. There were no marinas at the time and a favourite trip was the passage from our homeport of West Mersea up the Wallet, into Harwich Harbour and up the Orwell to anchor off Pin Mill. The Butt & Oyster pub was the place, a pint for dad, lemonade for me and back to the boat to cook dinner on a single burner primus stove. I can still smell the methylated spirit it needed to get started – magic!

'Sandora' was a nice old boat with a weedy three horse-power Stuart Turner engine, hand-cranked with a centrifugal clutch for ahead only. One day we approached the lock at Heybridge Basin near Maldon with a 25 knot wind from astern. So far so good, but how to stop? Dad went forward, boathook in hand, but of course it snapped like a carrot and our bowsprit rammed the lock gates like a jet carrier landing, much to the amusement of the locals.

The Kim Holman designed Stella burst on to the East Coast sailing scene for Burnham Week 1959 and won every race. The Tucker Brown yard in Burnham was building Stellas as fast as they could and by 1963 there was a growing fleet. The Stella was slightly bigger than a Folkboat, clinker built and with a little more freeboard. They were seaworthy and proven offshore, having already won several races on the East Anglian Offshore Racing Association (EAORA) circuit. I wanted to race and dad wanted a faster boat with a bit more space for cruising. The Stella was our ideal next boat.

We met the boss of Tucker Brown, Sonny Cole, who was a real character. He asked us if we could sail and then asked me if I could row properly. Yes, of course, I replied and he then pointed to a large yard dinghy tied to the end of their causeway and said, "See that red Stella on the moorings? She is unlocked. Go and have a sail, come back and tell me what you think." It would be hard to imagine a more laid-back sales pitch but I recall getting aboard for the first time and hearing that magic chuckle of water as the tide lapped on her clinker planking. Only those who have been aboard clinker-built boats will relate to this magical sound.

After a quick sail we were totally hooked but, as sailors on a budget, the Stella at £1,850 with sails and inboard engine was beyond our reach. Dad was the ultimate DIY guru so we agreed to buy an empty hull and deck, which we completed in the garden at West Mersea. I'd done a bit of offshore racing as crew but Stella 90 'Scorpio' gave me the opportunity, at the age of about 16, to skipper a competitive cruiser/racer.

My mates and I took to it like ducks to water, racing around the Thames Estuary and learning about the effect of tide and how to navigate, day and night, whenever we raced or wanted to cruise. There were so many great races, scooting along with our 3ft 10in draft in six feet or less of water, eyes on the sounder. Often, the larger faster boats would be in deeper water punching a foul tide and our tide dodging would enable us to match them boat for boat, building a nice time cushion on handicap.

There was also Stella class racing at Burnham where

The first 'UFO' (25.5ft) which led to the UFO 34 class and the start of Oyster Marine

a fleet of up to 35 boats would come together for Burnham Week. This was a real test, with a high standard of competition sailing against some real characters. The boat to beat was Gill Hedges' 'Lodestar' which in 57 starts one season won 52 races. As luck would have it, during our first Burnham Week in 'Scorpio', we were in the middle of the fleet beating to windward and hooked into a massive left-hand wind shift. It allowed us to get out of the strong spring ebb tide and more by luck than judgement gave us our first Stella class win.

We got better and over the years went on to top the Burnham Week Stella fleet seven or eight times. The class had its 50th anniversary in 2009 and 'Scorpio', now restored and in great condition, won the championship. So many of the deck and interior fittings were hand-made by my dad, while I used to skip college to do the painting. When my dad passed away, his ashes went over the side from 'Scorpio' with my children aboard. This is one boat that will stay in our family.

In 1972, John Harrison of Island Boat Sales loaned

me the first of class Hustler 25.5 which we named 'UFO'. We went on to win our class in the EAORA series and the following year won the championship overall. Next up I commissioned Holman & Pye to design a 32 footer, sized for Three Quarter Ton level rating and large enough to take part in the longer Royal Ocean Racing Club (RORC) offshore races. Like 'Scorpio' years before, we had a hull and deck built which we completed ourselves to contain cost. 'UFO 2' became the prototype of a production version, the UFO 34, and the start of Oyster Marine. (In 2004, 30 years later, we borrowed 'UFO 2' and returned to Burnham Week with the same crew and won the Commodore's Cup.)

Almost all our sailing took place on the East Coast with the magic of tides, estuaries and creeks making every sail unique. Over the 35 years or so that followed, Oyster, always East Coast based, became a global brand, winning two Queen's Awards and creating employment for over 600 people, but that's another story.

I've been lucky owning several lovely yachts, including a 12 Metre and "Kismet" a beautifully restored 50ft

'Kismet' in the West Mersea houseboat mud berths

The beautifully restored 'Kismet', 1898 Fife 50 footer

Fife from 1898. Do I have favourites? No, not really, as that would be like naming a favourite child. Sailing continues to be a driving passion and in recent years we have cruised to New Zealand, Alaska, the Arctic and lots of other wonderful places along the way.

Meanwhile, apart from the addition of a few marinas and a few wind farms, the East Coast is pretty much unchanged. Home is still West Mersea and I love to keep my yacht of the day on a swinging mooring, where we can enjoy a sunset over the anchorage with a chorus of seabirds. For me, that's the magic of the East Coast.

CHAPTER 16

The original Swatchways magician

Dick Durham recalls MG, the man and his legacy

Beneath some of the largest Scots pines on Mersea Island, Essex, sits the last 'cabin' of Maurice Griffiths. Severed from the mainland by a moat consisting of waters from the rivers Blackwater and Colne and the creeks of Pyefleet and Mersea Quarters, this humble bungalow is still just a stride away from a view of the forbidding black oyster shed which stands on stilts embedded in the saltings of Packing Marsh Island.

Dick at the helm of 'Nightfall', Maurice Griffiths' old Broads-built gaffer. She's been restored by marine artist Martyn Mackrill who keeps her at Yarmouth, Isle of Wight

The muddy sides of this marshy islet acted as Maurice's tide gauge. From the amount of glistening brown mud showing, he knew whether or not the Strood causeway linking Mersea with the rest of Essex was under water. He sensed relief when Packing Marsh Island told him he was marooned, for then he was back aboard the craft of his youth, isolated from the beck and call of daily life ashore.

The cabin was for Maurice both sanctuary and study. The cabin with its "all-pervading smell of damp bedding, wet sails, tarred rope, paraffin, dead stove ashes, trapped air and rusty bilge water" was transformed by the coal stove and the oil lamp into "the warmest and cosiest place imaginable". The cabin was the 'essence of yachting'.

His yacht 'Nightfall' had perhaps the best cabin he ever lived in. Lined with mahogany and beechwood panelling, a skylight sent down dusty shafts of sunlight on to a varnished leaf table. There was a figured carpet on the cabin sole that matched the red cushions and backrests over which carved rails "like miniature banisters" ran the length of the shelves. Above, mahogany coachroof beams "arched darkly against the white deckhead". On the after bulkhead a filigreed brass oil lamp used a mirror to double its illumination – a soft, warm light.

Such cabins are not created any more.

When the moat ebbs away and Mersea is reunited with Essex once more, the great sands of the Buxey and the Gunfleet rise from the sea. Though they muzzle the approaches to the Blackwater and Colne, they made Maurice feel secure. The peculiarity of the East Coaster is that, surrounded by sandbanks, he feels safe.

Maurice was a seaman who navigated by improvisation and initiative. The course marks on his charts would not necessarily have avoided hazards; more often than not they would have bisected them.

Such a sailor is a delta man and one of the greatest deltas criss-crossed by sailors in the UK is that found on the East Coast between Lowestoft and the North Foreland. Maurice Griffiths was a delta man, a man at home in the Thames Estuary.

"These anchorages in the Thames Estuary, where an expanse of drying sands can make a very useful harbour with the wind in the right direction, are naturally not so effective as a firm weather shore. Nevertheless even at high water they do calm down the seas to some extent."

That is the voice of the East Coaster, somebody at home sailing through a shallow maze.

The fug of fried eggs and bacon laced with coal smoke was just a memory as I sat in the cosy study of MG's home, yet there was a hint of the old magic still. It wasn't the brass oil lamp gleaming from the wall. Nor the half models of his successful designs hanging next to watercolours of his favourite yachts. Nor yet was it the leather-bound copies of 'Yachting Monthly', the magazine he edited for 40 years, lining the companionway which led out to the hall of his bungalow at West Mersea. It was to be many visits before I realised what spell it was that charmed me but gradually I came to understand my bewitching.

I noticed how often Maurice sat listening to my questions with his long, delicate fingers steepled under his chin. I noticed, too, how the cover was always off his typewriter and that invariably a sheet of paper was rolled in the carriage ready to take the patter of keys. It was the most significant object in that little room – his old-fashioned, sit-up-and-beg-style typewriter.

So I learned how Maurice himself sat up and via a succession of old portables begged a living with articles and literally wrote himself out of poverty. Also how, since then, he had never been without a trusty typewriter – neither ashore nor afloat.

It was as a teenager at home in Gippeswyk Avenue, Ipswich, that Maurice tentatively sent out articles about the local Orwell yacht races to the 'East Anglian Daily Times' to begin his writing career. A few publications encouraged him further – and Maurice was never a man who needed much encouragement – to write a little book on his experiences running a yacht agency. It was called 'Yachting on a Small Income'.

The year before this first book was published, 1925, his father Walter died suddenly and unexpectedly. Maurice was 22 years old when, along with his mother Lena, he was thrown out on to the streets. Walter had run up massive debts through gambling and womanising. The home, the furniture and Maurice's current boat, 'Storm', as well as the fledgling yacht agency he had begun, all had to be sold to pay off the bank.

His mother went to live with her sister in Lincolnshire. His brother, Leslie, was married with a son and lived in the far-away Midlands.

Maurice quickly weighed up the situation. Should he try to get a job on the local press or chance his arm in London on the nationals? He decided on the Dick Whittington route and soon regretted it.

Cooped up in damp bedsits around Euston, he batted away at his typewriter. By night, a sputtering gas ring gave him warmth as he wrote while, by day, he bravely touted his meticulously laid-out typescripts around busy and indifferent editorial offices.

One of the frustrations I faced over the hours spent with a tape-recorder, grilling Maurice about his long life, was trying to pin him down on absolutes. However, later as I flicked through back numbers of these yellowing magazines, I came to the conclusion it was an old habit that had kept him in bread and butter. Shrewdly, Maurice realised that definitive comment meant finite copy. If he condemned gaff against bermudian, hard chine against round bilge, clinker against carvel, he would soon have antifouled himself out of the boatyard.

Like those who can remember what they were doing when J F Kennedy was assassinated, I can recall where I was when first I came under that peculiar spell of Maurice's lyricism. It was in Aldeburgh in 1965 while thumbing through 'Magic of the Swatchways' in the mildewed yacht club library. I had sailed there on my father's Belouga 'Mouette'. He had gone off to pick up my mother and sister from the railway station so that we could all be together for a family holiday. While he was gone I slumped in a damp armchair and read about the voice of the shingle, the silent creeks.

By the time my father returned he had an incurable romantic for a crew.

Father, mother and sister took bed and breakfast in a local pub. I slept on board listening to the tide and dreaming of dangerous bars and friendly withies.

Maurice Griffiths could enslave a schoolboy with a few paragraphs about supper in a half-tide creek. Basil Lubbock had clippers foundering off Cape Horn and yet was still boring.

Maurice's prose has provided real comfort to many of his readers. The following came in a letter to me from one of his disciples as far away as New Zealand: "I have long lost count of the number of times I have read them all (his books) and I have always turned to them in times of stress or depression, particularly business worries, as the best means of relaxation and composure.

I think it is their aura of peace of mind and tranquillity that emanates from Maurice's descriptions that has the desired effect."

So when, 26 years later, I came to write Maurice Griffiths' biography, it was a slightly surreal experience to meet the man I felt I'd already known as a 14-year-old.

A light sou'westerly breeze was cracking the Terylene sails of dinghies about to be wheeled into the glittering summer tide as I drove to his new home, deliberately built up and away from the coast. He had not exactly turned his back on the waters from which he wrought a great career for, twice a month, he would drive down to West Mersea Yacht Club with his second wife, Coppie, for lunch. They took a table with a view over the Quarters. But it had inevitably changed.

As he observed after a display from some waterskiers on one of his last cruises to Hamford Water, in the Walton Backwaters, probably his best loved spot: "In comparison with noise-making sports like motorcycle racing, football, speedboating or even private flying, it is not necessarily a holier-than-thou attitude to think of small boat sailing and cruising as a form of pleasure that need cause no inconvenience to others.

"With your little home about you and the warm lamplight in the cabin inviting you below when the evening air begins to feel chilly, you have with you everything a man or woman may need to feel at peace with a world which at such times can seem far, far away."

By the time I came to meet the man himself his "little home" was permanently moored on dry land.

The door of his bungalow was open, letting in the warm summer air, when first I visited him in July 1991. A frail, spare man with a white, grizzled beard hiding the lantern jaw line of a still handsome face greeted me with shy, exquisite manners.

In his little shore-based cabin over the course of several months, I began asking the first questions about a life nearly 90 years old.

At last, when I felt I had exhausted my researches into the subject, I called in one day and told Maurice I had started writing and that as a result I felt a sense of relief. The articulate fingers steepled. The steady blue eyes fixed mine with a concentration built of long discipline. I wriggled. Out of habit Maurice moved his chair a little nearer his typewriter. "Yes," he said. "Starting a book is rather like priming a pump."

Dick Durham is news editor at 'Yachting Monthly' magazine. He is author of several East Coast books including his biography of Maurice Griffiths, 'The Magician of the Swatchways', published in 1994. This chapter is an abridged and slightly rewritten version of what appeared in Dick's original MG biography.

View across to the black oyster shed which stands on stilts on Packing Marsh Island, West Mersea